Schools Abroad is now the largest specialist ski tour operator in Great Britain, looking after 55,000 skiers in the 1979/80 season.
The company is principally engaged in organising holidays for parties of school children, although there is an increasing involvement in arranging budget holidays for adult skiers and families.
I feel sure that "Learning to Ski" will be an invaluable help in preparing you for your ski course, whatever your personal standard of skiing.
I hope that when you return from the snow the book will be useful as a souvenir, source of reference and permanent companion.

Peter Hopkins,
Managing Director,
Schools Abroad Ltd.

This book was created by
Chancerel Publishers Ltd for
Schools Abroad Ltd, Jubilee House,
Burgess Hill, West Sussex RH15 8DX.

Chancerel Publishers Ltd.
40 Tavistock Street,
London WC2E 7PB

ISBN 0-905703-49-9

Origination by ReproSharp, London, EC1
Printed in Italy

Acknowledgements
The author would like to thank Dennis Nelson for his assistance in the preparation of this book.

Photographs
Mervyn Rees: pages 16,30,39,51,62,76,80
John Shedden: pages 8,13,20,30,59,71,85
Don Morley (Allsport): front cover
Alpine Sports Ltd.: page 27
Rick Curthoys: Illustration pages 42–43

While every attempt has made to ensure that this book is accurate, the information it contains is of a general nature and not intended to represent the particular ski courses and tours arranged by Schools Abroad Ltd., full details of which are available in their current brochure.

LEARNING TO SKI

by John Shedden

Illustrations by Gerard Pestarque

schools abroad LIMITED

Contents

SKIING-PAST AND PRESENT

Today skiing is a thoroughbred sport with a world-wide following. Yet it began in prehistoric times in Scandinavia as a humble means of transport. Bronze Age hunters used short, wide skis made from local timber. And almost a thousand years ago Finnish, Russian and Norwegian Warriors used skis in war. Skiing as we know it today is scarcely a hundred years old and it owes its spectacular growth to a few people who contributed important developments. Sondre Nordheim produced the first bindings effective enough to permit a controlled turn — the telemark. Mathias Zardsky, an Austrian, wrote the first manual of ski technique and invented the snow-plough and stem turns. Sir Arnold Lunn invented slalom racing. Nowadays the sport of skiing is organised into two separate disciplines — Nordic, which includes cross-country and ski jumping, and Alpine or downhill racing.

A ski technique from the past being demonstrated to a modern audience.

From gliding Finns to modern resorts

THE SPORT OF SKIING IS 2,000 YEARS OLD. THE EARLIEST WRITTEN ACCOUNTS COME FROM PROCOPUIS (526-559AD). HE MENTIONED GLIDING FINNS — SKRIDFINER WHO RACED AGAINST NON-GLIDING FINNS.

TODAY OVER HALF A MILLION BRITONS TAKE TO THE SKI SLOPES OF BRITAIN AND EUROPE.

SKIING IS A RECREATION, SPORT AND EXERCISE IN AN ENVIRONMENT OF FRESH AIR AND FABULOUS SCENERY.

THE EXCITING MOUNTAIN ATMOSPHERE GIVES YOU A GREAT FEELING OF WELL-BEING.

The two disciplines—Nordic and Alpine

TODAY, THERE ARE TWO FORMS OF SKIING, NORDIC AND ALPINE.

IN BRITAIN AND EUROPE ALPINE, OR DOWNHILL, SKIING IS THE MOST POPULAR OF THE TWO DISCIPLINES.

FREESTYLE

NORDIC SKIING IS THE ORIGINAL FORM OF SKIING. IT CONSISTS OF LONG DISTANCE AND SPRINTING OVER RELATIVELY LEVEL TERRAIN . . .

. . . AND SKI JUMPING. THE SKIS ARE LONGER AND WIDER THAN ALPINE DESIGNS.

SLALOM AND DOWNHILL ARE THE MAIN FORMS OF COMPETITIVE SKIING. AND THERE IS ALSO FREESTYLE, WHICH INCLUDES BALLET.

Prehistoric skiing in Scandinavia

A SKI DUG UP BY ARCHAEOLOGISTS IN A PEAT BOG NEAR HOTING, SWEDEN, SHOWS THAT PEOPLE HAVE BEEN SKIING FOR ABOUT FOUR AND A HALF THOUSAND YEARS.

THE HOTING SKI IS WIDE AND SHORT AND MADE OF PINE. IT WAS USED MORE LIKE A SNOWSHOE THAN A MODERN SKI.

ROCK DRAWINGS OF SKIS DATED 2,500 BC HAVE BEEN FOUND IN NORWAY.

ONE ROCK INSCRIPTION SHOWS WHAT COULD BE A HUNTER IN ACTION ON SKIS.

Skis for mountain transport

THE WORD SKI SEEMS TO HAVE COME FROM SCANDINAVIA, MEANING TO SKID

CENTRAL NORDIC SKIS WERE OF UNEQUAL LENGTH. THE SKIIER SCOOTED OR SKATED WITH THE SHORTER SKI, HELPED BY A LONG POLE, AND GLIDED ON THE LONGER SKI.

HUNTERS CONTINUED TO USE SKIS TO GET AROUND IN THE LONG NORTHERN WINTER, AS SHOWN IN THIS SIXTEENTH CENTURY ILLUSTRATION.

SCANDINAVIAN ARMIES USED SKIS EXTENSIVELY ON THE BATTLEFIELD.

How skiing competitions began

THE FIRST SLALOM COMPETITIONS WERE HELD AT MURREN, IN SWITZERLAND IN 1922.

THE FIRST MODERN SKIING COMPETITIONS TOOK PLACE IN 1866 IN KRISTIANIA, NOW CALLED OSLO, THE CAPITAL OF NORWAY. THE EVENTS INCLUDED JUMPING AND DISTANCE RACES.

AN ENGLISHMAN, SIR ARNOLD LUNN, INVENTED SLALOM RACING.

Development of skiing techniques

MANY PEOPLE HAVE CONTRIBUTED TO THE DEVELOPMENT OF SKIING AS A SPORT.

IN FACT NORDHEIM'S TECHNIQUES WERE THE BASIS OF SKIING IN EUROPE AND THE U.S.A. FROM 1870-1910.

MATHIAS ZDARSKY FROM AUSTRIA MADE SHORTER SKIS AND METAL BINDINGS, FROM WHICH MODERN EQUIPMENT HAS BEEN DEVELOPED, FOR CONTROLLED SKIING ON THE STEEPER ALPINE TERRAIN.

SONDRE NORDHEIM, A NORWEGIAN, INVENTED A SKI BINDING, WHICH FIXED THE BOOTS FIRMLY TO THE SKIS . . .

LILIENFELDER SKI TECHNIQUE
MATHIAS ZDARSKY.
1896

HE WROTE THE FIRST KNOWN BOOK DESCRIBING EQUIPMENT AND TECHNIQUE CALLED 'LILIENFELDER SKI TECHNIQUE."

. . . AND ALSO THE TELEMARK TURN, AN IMPORTANT ADVANCE IN TECHNIQUE.

Modern skiing events

Competition exists at all levels of skiing, from local club events to the Olympic Games, or the World Cup. If you wish to race, you will be able to do so on artificial slopes in Britain, and probably there will be the opportunity to join visitors' races on your holiday or ski course.

Special slalom

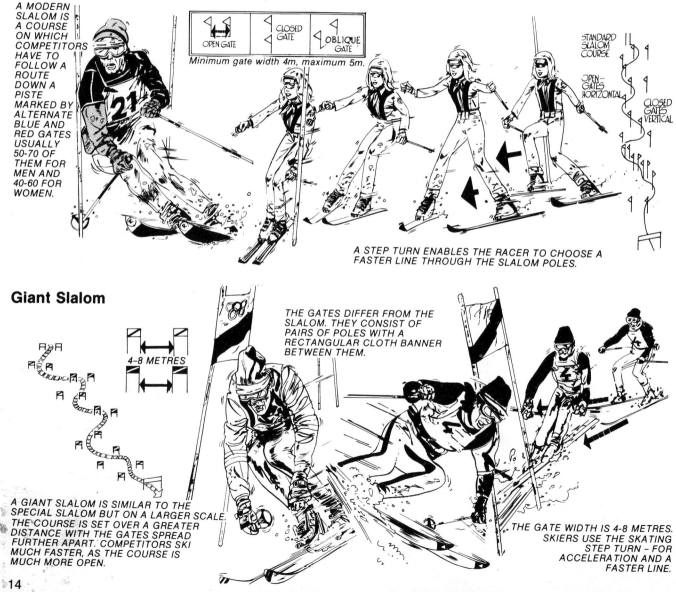

A MODERN SLALOM IS A COURSE ON WHICH COMPETITORS HAVE TO FOLLOW A ROUTE DOWN A PISTE MARKED BY ALTERNATE BLUE AND RED GATES USUALLY 50-70 OF THEM FOR MEN AND 40-60 FOR WOMEN.

Minimum gate width 4m, maximum 5m.

OPEN GATE   CLOSED GATE   OBLIQUE GATE

STANDARD SLALOM COURSE

OPEN GATES HORIZONTAL

CLOSED GATES VERTICAL

A STEP TURN ENABLES THE RACER TO CHOOSE A FASTER LINE THROUGH THE SLALOM POLES.

Giant Slalom

4-8 METRES

THE GATES DIFFER FROM THE SLALOM. THEY CONSIST OF PAIRS OF POLES WITH A RECTANGULAR CLOTH BANNER BETWEEN THEM.

A GIANT SLALOM IS SIMILAR TO THE SPECIAL SLALOM BUT ON A LARGER SCALE. THE COURSE IS SET OVER A GREATER DISTANCE WITH THE GATES SPREAD FURTHER APART. COMPETITORS SKI MUCH FASTER, AS THE COURSE IS MUCH MORE OPEN.

THE GATE WIDTH IS 4-8 METRES. SKIERS USE THE SKATING STEP TURN - FOR ACCELERATION AND A FASTER LINE.

14

Downhill

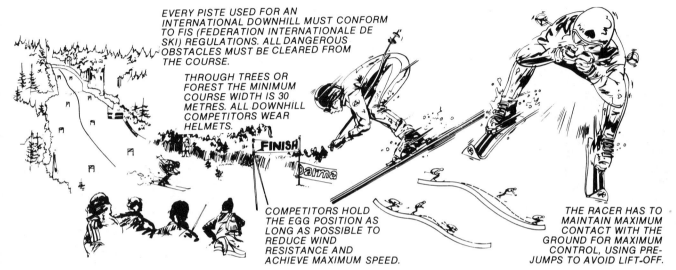

EVERY PISTE USED FOR AN INTERNATIONAL DOWNHILL MUST CONFORM TO FIS (FEDERATION INTERNATIONALE DE SKI) REGULATIONS. ALL DANGEROUS OBSTACLES MUST BE CLEARED FROM THE COURSE.

THROUGH TREES OR FOREST THE MINIMUM COURSE WIDTH IS 30 METRES. ALL DOWNHILL COMPETITORS WEAR HELMETS.

FINISH

palma

COMPETITORS HOLD THE EGG POSITION AS LONG AS POSSIBLE TO REDUCE WIND RESISTANCE AND ACHIEVE MAXIMUM SPEED.

THE RACER HAS TO MAINTAIN MAXIMUM CONTACT WITH THE GROUND FOR MAXIMUM CONTROL, USING PRE-JUMPS TO AVOID LIFT-OFF.

Freestyle

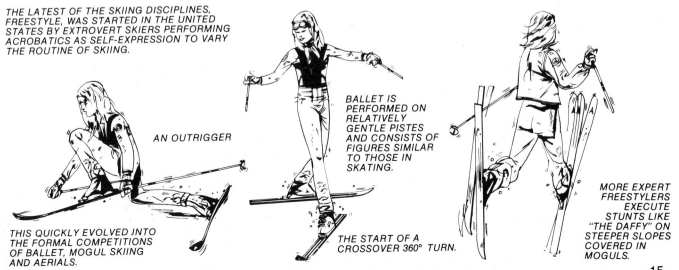

THE LATEST OF THE SKIING DISCIPLINES, FREESTYLE, WAS STARTED IN THE UNITED STATES BY EXTROVERT SKIERS PERFORMING ACROBATICS AS SELF-EXPRESSION TO VARY THE ROUTINE OF SKIING.

AN OUTRIGGER

BALLET IS PERFORMED ON RELATIVELY GENTLE PISTES AND CONSISTS OF FIGURES SIMILAR TO THOSE IN SKATING.

MORE EXPERT FREESTYLERS EXECUTE STUNTS LIKE "THE DAFFY" ON STEEPER SLOPES COVERED IN MOGULS.

THIS QUICKLY EVOLVED INTO THE FORMAL COMPETITIONS OF BALLET, MOGUL SKIING AND AERIALS.

THE START OF A CROSSOVER 360° TURN.

Aerials

MANY FREESTYLE COMPETITORS ALSO PERFORM AERIALS AS A SPECIFIC EVENT.

THERE ARE THREE KINDS OF AERIALS – INVERSIONS, SPINS AND UPRIGHTS.

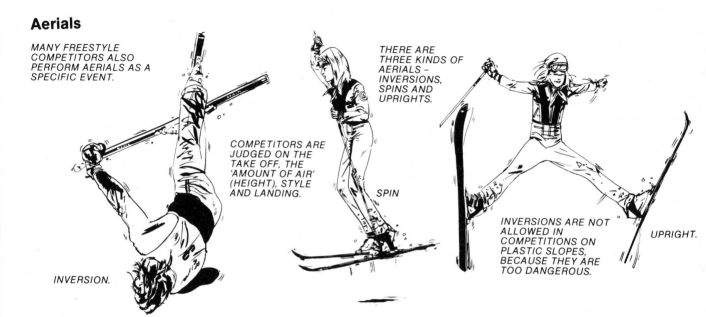

COMPETITORS ARE JUDGED ON THE TAKE OFF, THE 'AMOUNT OF AIR' (HEIGHT), STYLE AND LANDING.

SPIN

INVERSIONS ARE NOT ALLOWED IN COMPETITIONS ON PLASTIC SLOPES, BECAUSE THEY ARE TOO DANGEROUS.

UPRIGHT.

INVERSION.

Ski touring

FOR SKI TOURING AS A SPORT YOU MUST LEAVE THE PISTE AND SET OFF TO EXPLORE THE MOUNTAINS.

DON'T FORGET TO TAKE A RUCKSACK WITH EMERGENCY PROVISIONS.

THE FAMOUS HIGH ROUTE . . .

. . . FROM CHAMONIX TO ZERMATT IS ONE OF THE BEST SKI TOURS IN EUROPE . . .

. . . INVOLVING OVERNIGHT STAYS AT MOUNTAIN HUTS. BUT IT IS DONE WITH A GUIDE.

CROSS COUNTRY SKIERS USE SYNTHETIC "SKINS" TO PREVENT THE SKIS GOING BACKWARDS, SO THAT THEY CAN WALK.

Ski jumping

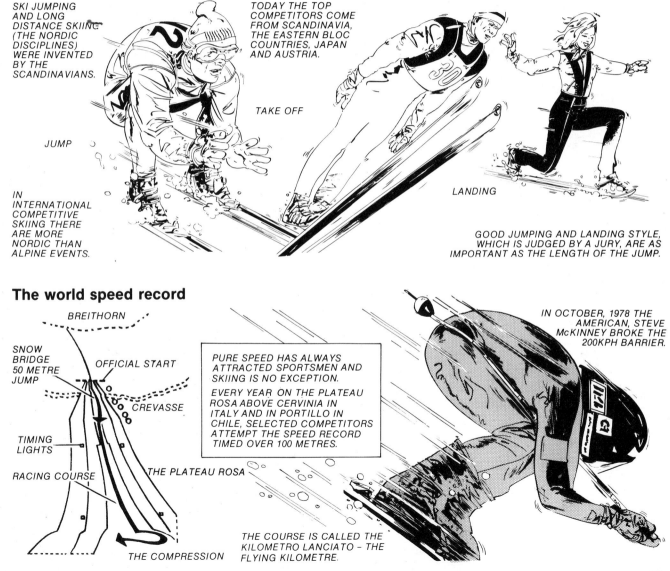

SKI JUMPING AND LONG DISTANCE SKIING (THE NORDIC DISCIPLINES) WERE INVENTED BY THE SCANDINAVIANS.

TODAY THE TOP COMPETITORS COME FROM SCANDINAVIA, THE EASTERN BLOC COUNTRIES, JAPAN AND AUSTRIA.

JUMP

TAKE OFF

LANDING

IN INTERNATIONAL COMPETITIVE SKIING THERE ARE MORE NORDIC THAN ALPINE EVENTS.

GOOD JUMPING AND LANDING STYLE, WHICH IS JUDGED BY A JURY, ARE AS IMPORTANT AS THE LENGTH OF THE JUMP.

The world speed record

BREITHORN

SNOW BRIDGE 50 METRE JUMP

OFFICIAL START

CREVASSE

TIMING LIGHTS

RACING COURSE

THE PLATEAU ROSA

THE COMPRESSION

PURE SPEED HAS ALWAYS ATTRACTED SPORTSMEN AND SKIING IS NO EXCEPTION.

EVERY YEAR ON THE PLATEAU ROSA ABOVE CERVINIA IN ITALY AND IN PORTILLO IN CHILE, SELECTED COMPETITORS ATTEMPT THE SPEED RECORD TIMED OVER 100 METRES.

IN OCTOBER, 1978 THE AMERICAN, STEVE McKINNEY BROKE THE 200KPH BARRIER.

THE COURSE IS CALLED THE KILOMETRO LANCIATO – THE FLYING KILOMETRE.

KNOW YOUR EQUIPMENT

Skiing is an activity which requires very special equipment. Skis are sophisticated tools and must be treated with care, if they are to function properly. Clothing must permit comfortable and easy movement and yet should protect you against the weather in the mountains. You may meet blizzards or extremes of temperature at high altitudes. Your boots must be comfortable if you are to ski well. Many new skiers don't progress as fast as they could because they have ill-fitting equipment. If your skis are modern they are likely to be made to recent designs that suit all conditions.

To be safe in the mountains you must have good equipment and wear the right clothes — not necessarily the most fashionable ones.

Bright colours of children's ski clothing at Kitzbühel, Austria.

All about boots

In the last few years there has been a revolution in boot design. Now they are usually made of thermo-setting plastics or polyurethane, with a flow fitting interior, which moulds to the shape of your foot as it warms up. If you are buying boots, do so before you go and wear them in the shop for at least 15 minutes, to allow the flow-fit to work.

Alpine ski boots

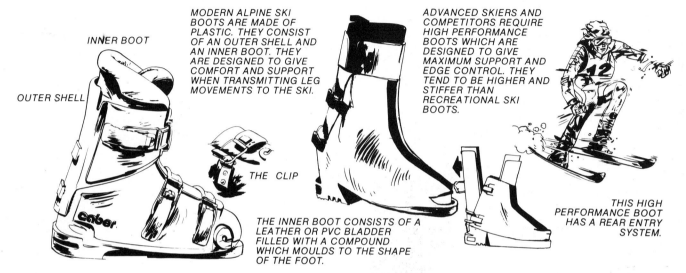

INNER BOOT

OUTER SHELL

MODERN ALPINE SKI BOOTS ARE MADE OF PLASTIC. THEY CONSIST OF AN OUTER SHELL AND AN INNER BOOT. THEY ARE DESIGNED TO GIVE COMFORT AND SUPPORT WHEN TRANSMITTING LEG MOVEMENTS TO THE SKI.

THE CLIP

THE INNER BOOT CONSISTS OF A LEATHER OR PVC BLADDER FILLED WITH A COMPOUND WHICH MOULDS TO THE SHAPE OF THE FOOT.

ADVANCED SKIERS AND COMPETITORS REQUIRE HIGH PERFORMANCE BOOTS WHICH ARE DESIGNED TO GIVE MAXIMUM SUPPORT AND EDGE CONTROL. THEY TEND TO BE HIGHER AND STIFFER THAN RECREATIONAL SKI BOOTS.

THIS HIGH PERFORMANCE BOOT HAS A REAR ENTRY SYSTEM.

Fitting your boots

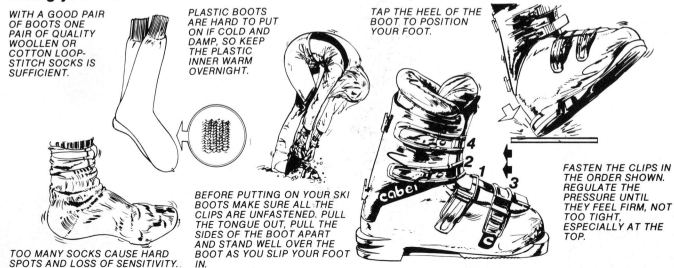

WITH A GOOD PAIR OF BOOTS ONE PAIR OF QUALITY WOOLLEN OR COTTON LOOP-STITCH SOCKS IS SUFFICIENT.

PLASTIC BOOTS ARE HARD TO PUT ON IF COLD AND DAMP, SO KEEP THE PLASTIC INNER WARM OVERNIGHT.

TAP THE HEEL OF THE BOOT TO POSITION YOUR FOOT.

TOO MANY SOCKS CAUSE HARD SPOTS AND LOSS OF SENSITIVITY.

BEFORE PUTTING ON YOUR SKI BOOTS MAKE SURE ALL THE CLIPS ARE UNFASTENED. PULL THE TONGUE OUT, PULL THE SIDES OF THE BOOT APART AND STAND WELL OVER THE BOOT AS YOU SLIP YOUR FOOT IN.

FASTEN THE CLIPS IN THE ORDER SHOWN. REGULATE THE PRESSURE UNTIL THEY FEEL FIRM, NOT TOO TIGHT, ESPECIALLY AT THE TOP.

Checking the fit

FOR COMFORT AND GOOD SKIING IT IS ESSENTIAL TO HAVE BOOTS THAT FIT YOU.

WHEN YOUR BOOTS ARE FASTENED, YOU SHOULD NOT BE ABLE TO LIFT YOUR HEEL MORE THAN ½ inch.

CHECK YOUR CONTINENTAL BOOT SIZE.

IF YOU STAND ON YOUR TOES YOUR FOOT SHOULD NOT SLIDE FORWARDS INSIDE THE BOOT.

A LOOSE BOOT WILL RUB AND GIVE YOU BLISTERS. A TIGHT BOOT WILL CONSTRICT YOUR FOOT AND MAY CAUSE CRAMP.

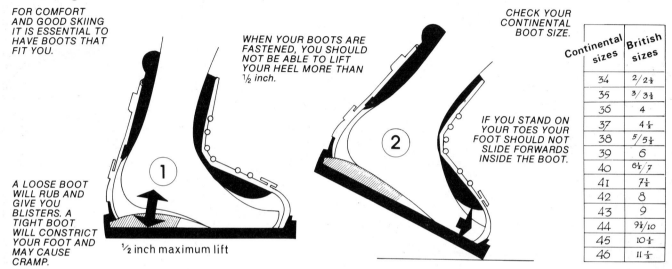

½ inch maximum lift

Continental sizes	British sizes
34	2/2½
35	3/3½
36	4
37	4½
38	5/5½
39	6
40	6½/7
41	7½
42	8
43	9
44	9½/10
45	10½
46	11½

Walking in ski boots

SKI BOOTS ARE AWKWARD TO WALK IN, BECAUSE THEY DO NOT FLEX LIKE SHOES. SOME MODERN BOOTS HAVE A HINGE TO HELP WITH FORWARD MOVEMENT, WHILE REMAINING RIGID LATERALLY.

TRY TO AVOID WALKING ON HARD SURFACES, WHICH WEAR THE TOES AND HEELS, GIVING YOU "BANANA BOOTS".

HINGE

UNDOING THE TOP CLIP ONLY WILL HELP YOU WALK IN SKI BOOTS.

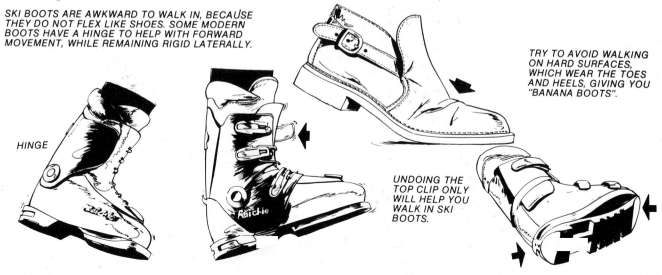

Bindings and ski sticks

There are many types of release bindings, which attach your boot to the ski. They are mostly of the step-in or plate design. Both are relatively safe if correctly adjusted for your weight, height, strength and ability. Make sure they are properly adjusted in the hire shop, before you ski.

Release bindings

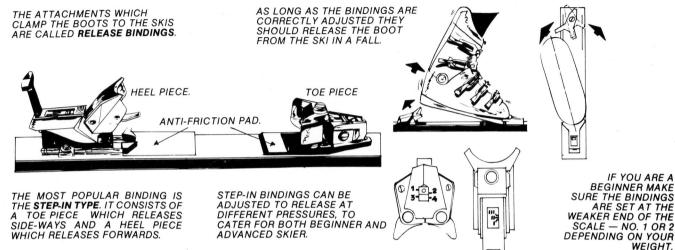

THE ATTACHMENTS WHICH CLAMP THE BOOTS TO THE SKIS ARE CALLED **RELEASE BINDINGS**.

AS LONG AS THE BINDINGS ARE CORRECTLY ADJUSTED THEY SHOULD RELEASE THE BOOT FROM THE SKI IN A FALL.

HEEL PIECE.

TOE PIECE

ANTI-FRICTION PAD.

THE MOST POPULAR BINDING IS THE **STEP-IN TYPE**. IT CONSISTS OF A TOE PIECE WHICH RELEASES SIDE-WAYS AND A HEEL PIECE WHICH RELEASES FORWARDS.

STEP-IN BINDINGS CAN BE ADJUSTED TO RELEASE AT DIFFERENT PRESSURES, TO CATER FOR BOTH BEGINNER AND ADVANCED SKIER.

IF YOU ARE A BEGINNER MAKE SURE THE BINDINGS ARE SET AT THE WEAKER END OF THE SCALE — NO. 1 OR 2 DEPENDING ON YOUR WEIGHT.

Choosing the right length of ski sticks

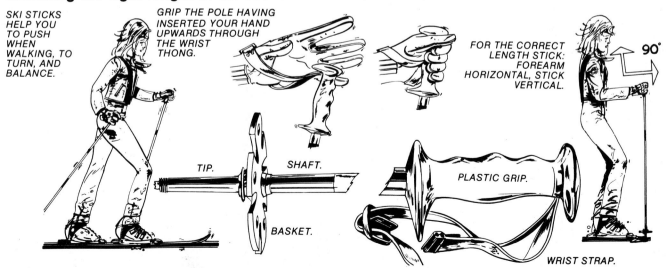

SKI STICKS HELP YOU TO PUSH WHEN WALKING, TO TURN, AND BALANCE.

GRIP THE POLE HAVING INSERTED YOUR HAND UPWARDS THROUGH THE WRIST THONG.

FOR THE CORRECT LENGTH STICK: FOREARM HORIZONTAL, STICK VERTICAL.

90°

TIP.

SHAFT.

PLASTIC GRIP.

BASKET.

WRIST STRAP.

Stepping off to one side at the top of a T-bar lift.

Ski clothing

Skiers are very fashion conscious. But beware! Fashionable ski wear is not always the warmest and the best. Sitting stranded on a broken chair lift is cold comfort for those who choose unwisely.

The only way to choose ski clothes is by their warmth and their fit. You may well run into sub-zero temperatures and blizzards, and then your clothes must give you good insulation. And when you are skiing energetically, your clothes must allow you generous freedom of movement.

As far as insulation is concerned, the different materials available vary enormously. Quilted clothes are warmer than non-quilted, because warm air is trapped between the layers. Duck down is warmest of all, but it is also the most expensive and it suffers badly in the wet. New synthetics, such as Hollofill, are cheaper, lighter, almost as warm and can even be washed.

You can hire ski wear if you wish to, but if you are likely to be going more than once, it is worth buying. Some people improvise, using anoraks they may have already, which is fine except that normal clothes are seldom warm enough for skiing. You may also be able to borrow, or share with friends who are not going this year or going at different times.

SOCKS Try to avoid wearing more than one pair. With modern boots one pair of cotton or wool 3/4-length, loop-stitch socks is quite adequate. Poor circulation? Cold feet? Try a pair of silk socks plus a pair of loop-stitch.

UNDER GARMENTS Clothes worn under your jacket and trousers. The number and type of under garments to wear depends on the weather and how much energy you are using.

You may feel adequately clothed while skiing, but unprotected during periods of inactivity on a ski tow, in a ski class, or on a chair lift. If you venture up the mountain never leave your ski jacket behind! Temperature **decreases** as altitude and wind strength increase. Take the following to protect you from the worst conditions:

For Your Legs
Tights or long thermal underwear
For Your Upper Body
Thin cotton vests; a high necked cotton or woollen sweater; a thin woollen sweater; a thick woollen sweater.

OUTER GARMENTS
Outer garments are your ski jacket, pants, salopettes and ski suit. These should be windproof, water resistant, (not necessarily waterproof, as this causes condensation from perspiration) and made of anti-gliss fabric.

Jacket
1. Choose anti-gliss material.
2. Choose a jacket that is long enough to overlap the top of your ski pants by 4—6 ins, at least.
3. Look for a high collar.
4. Good thermal filling with minimum cold spots.
5. Close fitting cuffs, neck and bottom to keep snow out.
6. Good quality, heavy duty zips.
7. Hood stored inside neck of jacket.
8. Window for ski pass.

Ski Pants
Basically there are three styles of ski pants.
1. Type worn inside the boot with a strap under the foot. Not a good design as snow gets in and causes blisters with modern close-fitting boot.
2. Loose flares worn over the boot with an insert to stop snow entering.
3. Racing style, close fitting over the boots attached to the top clips with zips at the back.

Salopettes
These are usually worn with a jacket as a ski suit. They are made of stetch or quilted material with synthetic fibre. They tend to be warmer because they cover the midriff and kidney region. Look for wide adjustable shoulder straps for maximum comfort.

Gloves or Mittens
Mittens tend to keep the hands warmer than gloves but gloves give greater range of movement and grip on the sticks. As beginners do not need to use their sticks as much as experts mittens will suffice. Gloves and mittens are made of a variety of materials which include plastic, nylon and leather or a combination of two materials. The cheaper type tend to be vinyl and quilted nylon, whereas leather is the most expensive. A pair of leather gloves with silk linings give the most warmth and freedom of movement. Good gloves are better than good mittens, but good mittens are better than poor gloves.

Ski clothes, can be fashionable and effective, But if you have to choose, make sure they are warm rather than smart.

All about skis

There are several things to check on when you are hiring skis. Make sure there are no holes or large gouges in the sole of the ski. If the skis are made of wood, make sure that the laminations are not separating, or warping. If conditions are icy, you may need the edges sharpened. If the snow is wet, you may need to apply special ski wax.

Ski terminology

HERE ARE THE NAMES OF THE MAIN PARTS OF A SKI

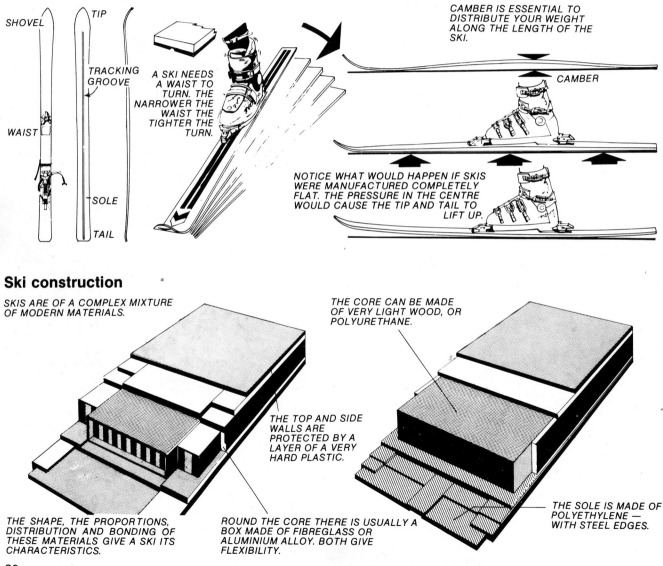

SHOVEL

TIP

TRACKING GROOVE

WAIST

SOLE

TAIL

A SKI NEEDS A WAIST TO TURN. THE NARROWER THE WAIST THE TIGHTER THE TURN.

CAMBER IS ESSENTIAL TO DISTRIBUTE YOUR WEIGHT ALONG THE LENGTH OF THE SKI.

CAMBER

NOTICE WHAT WOULD HAPPEN IF SKIS WERE MANUFACTURED COMPLETELY FLAT. THE PRESSURE IN THE CENTRE WOULD CAUSE THE TIP AND TAIL TO LIFT UP.

Ski construction

SKIS ARE OF A COMPLEX MIXTURE OF MODERN MATERIALS.

THE CORE CAN BE MADE OF VERY LIGHT WOOD, OR POLYURETHANE.

THE TOP AND SIDE WALLS ARE PROTECTED BY A LAYER OF A VERY HARD PLASTIC.

THE SHAPE, THE PROPORTIONS, DISTRIBUTION AND BONDING OF THESE MATERIALS GIVE A SKI ITS CHARACTERISTICS.

ROUND THE CORE THERE IS USUALLY A BOX MADE OF FIBREGLASS OR ALUMINIUM ALLOY. BOTH GIVE FLEXIBILITY.

THE SOLE IS MADE OF POLYETHYLENE — WITH STEEL EDGES.

Choosing the right length of ski

IDEALLY SKIS FOR THE BEGINNER SHOULD BE BETWEEN CHIN AND EYE HEIGHT, ALTHOUGH SOME SMALL COMPROMISE MAY BE NECESSARY.

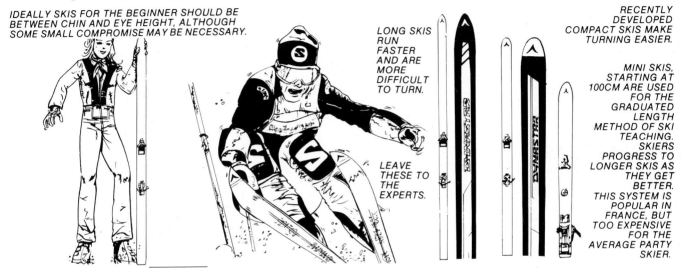

LONG SKIS RUN FASTER AND ARE MORE DIFFICULT TO TURN.

LEAVE THESE TO THE EXPERTS.

RECENTLY DEVELOPED COMPACT SKIS MAKE TURNING EASIER.

MINI SKIS, STARTING AT 100CM ARE USED FOR THE GRADUATED LENGTH METHOD OF SKI TEACHING. SKIERS PROGRESS TO LONGER SKIS AS THEY GET BETTER. THIS SYSTEM IS POPULAR IN FRANCE, BUT TOO EXPENSIVE FOR THE AVERAGE PARTY SKIER.

Carrying your skis

SKIS ARE AWKWARD TO CARRY AND CAN BE DANGEROUS, IF YOU ARE NOT CAREFUL.

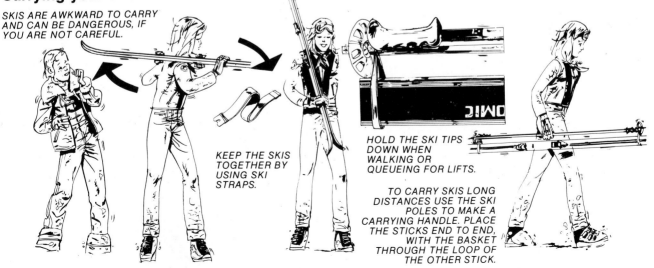

KEEP THE SKIS TOGETHER BY USING SKI STRAPS.

HOLD THE SKI TIPS DOWN WHEN WALKING OR QUEUEING FOR LIFTS.

TO CARRY SKIS LONG DISTANCES USE THE SKI POLES TO MAKE A CARRYING HANDLE. PLACE THE STICKS END TO END, WITH THE BASKET THROUGH THE LOOP OF THE OTHER STICK.

ONTO THE SLOPES

A fair amount of preparation goes into learning to ski. Unless you are lucky enough to live in the mountains, you cannot just don skis and glide away. First you must choose your resort. Does it have the kind of facilities you want? If you are just beginning you will need good nursery slopes with a reliable snow record. Next, what kind of lifts are there and do you know how to use them? And what should you do when, like many others, you fall off a drag lift? Knowing these things and a few simple safety rules, you will be that much better equiped to tackle the slopes. Mountains can be dangerous places, so find out what the piste signs mean, if they are not in English, and remember the main points of the Ski-way Code: the slower skier has right of way; overtake uphill, as wide as possible; if you fall, move off the piste; stop and offer help if there's an accident.

Crisp air and hot sun during a break in the day's skiing. Take care to avoid sunburn.

Weather conditions for skiing

MOUNTAIN WEATHER CONDITIONS CAN VARY FROM EXTREMES OF COLD WITH BLIZZARDS...

...TO BRIGHT SUNSHINE AND CLEAR BLUE SKIES.

BE READY TO MEET ALL CONDITIONS. YOU COULD SUFFER FROM EXPOSURE OR SUNBURN! PROTECT YOURSELF WITH WELL DESIGNED WARM CLOTHING, GOGGLES, GLOVES, SUNGLASSES AND SUNCREAMS.

PLAINS   MOUNTAINS

A WARM GENTLE WIND ON THE PLAINS BECOMES MUCH STRONGER AND COLDER WHEN IT IS FORCED UP OVER THE MOUNTAINS.

28

Snow conditions

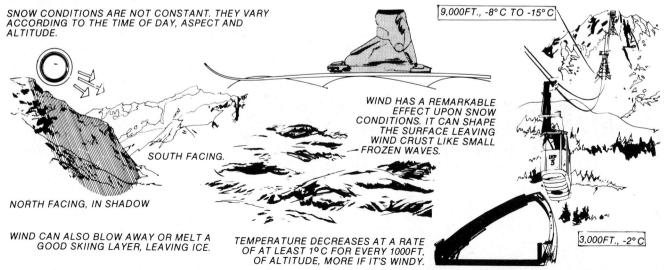

SNOW CONDITIONS ARE NOT CONSTANT. THEY VARY ACCORDING TO THE TIME OF DAY, ASPECT AND ALTITUDE.

SOUTH FACING.

NORTH FACING, IN SHADOW

WIND CAN ALSO BLOW AWAY OR MELT A GOOD SKIING LAYER, LEAVING ICE.

WIND HAS A REMARKABLE EFFECT UPON SNOW CONDITIONS. IT CAN SHAPE THE SURFACE LEAVING WIND CRUST LIKE SMALL FROZEN WAVES.

9,000FT., -8°C TO -15°C

TEMPERATURE DECREASES AT A RATE OF AT LEAST 1°C FOR EVERY 1000FT. OF ALTITUDE, MORE IF IT'S WINDY.

3,000FT., -2°C

The sun and snow

AT HIGH ALTITUDE THE FIERCENESS OF THE SUN INCREASES. YOU WILL NEED TO PROTECT YOURSELF FROM ULTRA VIOLET LIGHT AND GLARE, AS THE INTENSITY OF THE SUN IS REFLECTED OFF THE SNOW.

YOU WILL NEED HIGH PROTECTION (FACTOR 4 TO 6) CREAMS TO PROTECT YOUR SKIN FROM BLISTERING.

AND GOGGLES OR SUN GLASSES TO COMBAT THE GLARE. USE YELLOW LENSES IN BAD LIGHT.

Piste maintenance

THE SKI RESORT AUTHORITIES WILL PREPARE AND MAINTAIN THE PISTES.

IF THERE IS A SHORTAGE OF SNOW, BUT IT IS BELOW FREEZING, IT IS POSSIBLE TO USE SNOW-MAKING MACHINES.

THEY USE TRACKED SNOW CATS TO COMPACT NEW SNOW, MARK OUT THE TRAILS, AND FLATTEN MOGULS THAT HAVE HAVE BECOME TOO STEEP AND ICY.

THE SKI PATROL IS RESPONSIBLE FOR MONITORING AVALANCHES AND TENDING TO INJURED SKIERS. THEY GENERALLY MAKE SURE THE PISTES ARE AS SAFE AS POSSIBLE.

LATE IN THE DAY THE SKI PATROL CHECK THAT NO-ONE IS LEFT ON THE MOUNTAIN.

Uphill travel

It is normally cheaper to buy your ski lift pass using the special rates negotiated by the tour operator. If you think that you will be on the nursery slopes all week, then a points ticket may be cheaper. However, bear in mind that snow conditions may change, making the use of the upper slopes a necessity.

Types of ski lift

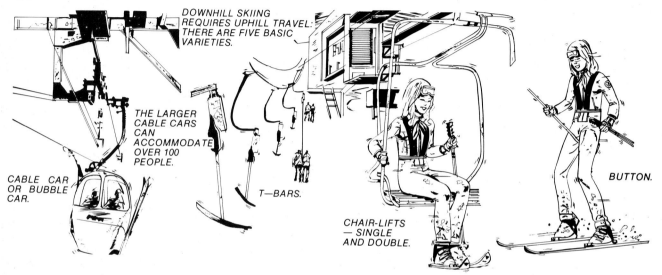

DOWNHILL SKIING REQUIRES UPHILL TRAVEL: THERE ARE FIVE BASIC VARIETIES.

THE LARGER CABLE CARS CAN ACCOMMODATE OVER 100 PEOPLE.

CABLE CAR OR BUBBLE CAR.

T—BARS.

CHAIR-LIFTS — SINGLE AND DOUBLE.

BUTTON.

Learning to ride a ski tow

WHEN YOU HAVE LEARNED TO TURN (USUALLY ON THE SECOND OR THIRD DAY), IT'S TIME TO TAKE THE SKI TOW UP THE MOUNTAIN.

GET READY **BEFORE** YOU ACCEPT THE TOW FROM THE ATTENDANT.

IF IT'S A BUTTON TOW, HANG YOUR SKI STICKS FROM ONE WRIST BY THEIR STRAPS.

STAND WITH YOUR SKIS PARALLEL ABOUT 1FT. (30CMS) APART.

FLEX THE LEGS, BALANCING OVER THE BALLS OF YOUR FEET.

TAKE THE BAR, PUT THE BUTTON BETWEEN YOUR LEGS AND FEEL THAT IT IS PUSHING YOU FROM BEHIND.

34

Riding the ruts and bumps

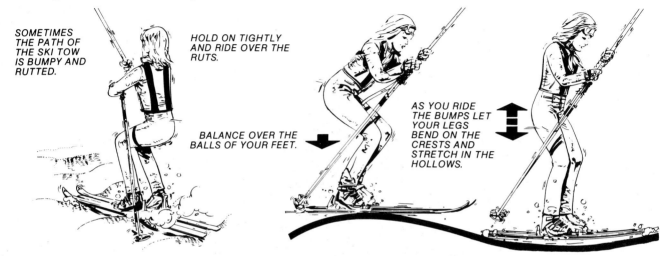

SOMETIMES THE PATH OF THE SKI TOW IS BUMPY AND RUTTED.

HOLD ON TIGHTLY AND RIDE OVER THE RUTS.

BALANCE OVER THE BALLS OF YOUR FEET.

AS YOU RIDE THE BUMPS LET YOUR LEGS BEND ON THE CRESTS AND STRETCH IN THE HOLLOWS.

What to do if you fall off

IF YOU OVERBALANCE OR FALL OFF THE SKI TOW, DON'T HANG ON — LET GO AND MOVE QUICKLY TO THE SIDE TO AVOID A COLLISION WITH THE PERSON FOLLOWING.

—OR WALK DOWN TO THE BOTTOM OF THE SKI TOW AND WAIT UNTIL YOUR CLASS ARRIVES.

IF YOU FALL HALF WAY UP THE SKI TOW YOU HAVE TWO CHOICES:

—EITHER TAKE YOUR SKIS OFF AND MAKE YOUR WAY TO THE PISTE AND WAIT THERE FOR YOUR INSTRUCTOR TO COLLECT YOU ON THE WAY DOWN.

WHEN YOU TAKE YOUR SKIS OFF BE CAREFUL NOT TO LOSE A SKI DOWN THE MOUNTAIN.

Releasing the tow at the top

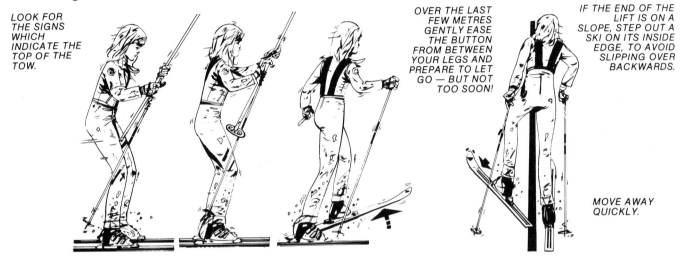

LOOK FOR THE SIGNS WHICH INDICATE THE TOP OF THE TOW.

OVER THE LAST FEW METRES GENTLY EASE THE BUTTON FROM BETWEEN YOUR LEGS AND PREPARE TO LET GO — BUT NOT TOO SOON!

IF THE END OF THE LIFT IS ON A SLOPE, STEP OUT A SKI ON ITS INSIDE EDGE, TO AVOID SLIPPING OVER BACKWARDS.

MOVE AWAY QUICKLY.

Chair lifts

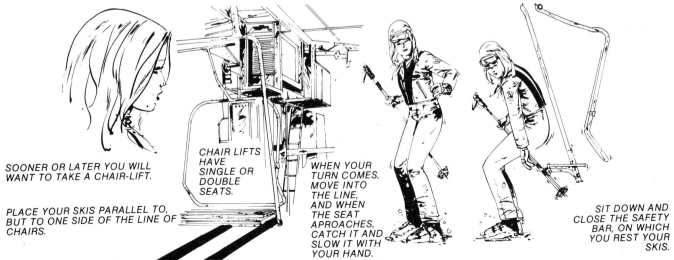

SOONER OR LATER YOU WILL WANT TO TAKE A CHAIR-LIFT.

PLACE YOUR SKIS PARALLEL TO, BUT TO ONE SIDE OF THE LINE OF CHAIRS.

CHAIR LIFTS HAVE SINGLE OR DOUBLE SEATS.

WHEN YOUR TURN COMES, MOVE INTO THE LINE, AND WHEN THE SEAT APPROACHES, CATCH IT AND SLOW IT WITH YOUR HAND.

SIT DOWN AND CLOSE THE SAFETY BAR, ON WHICH YOU REST YOUR SKIS.

37

Leaving the chair lift

NOW TO GET OFF THE CHAIR LIFT.

...PUSH YOURSELF OFF THE SEAT, AND STAND UP FORWARDS.

SKI DOWN THE RAMP WHICH WILL GUIDE YOU AWAY FROM THE CHAIRS.

AS SOON AS YOU COME LEVEL WITH THE LAST PYLON, OPEN THE SAFETY BAR AND WHEN YOUR SKIS MAKE CONTACT WITH THE SNOW...

Piste signs

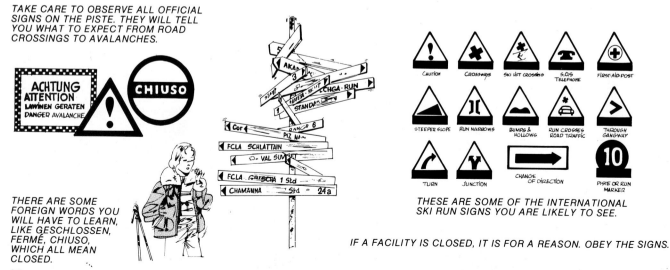

TAKE CARE TO OBSERVE ALL OFFICIAL SIGNS ON THE PISTE. THEY WILL TELL YOU WHAT TO EXPECT FROM ROAD CROSSINGS TO AVALANCHES.

ACHTUNG ATTENTION LAWINEN GERATEN DANGER AVALANCHE

CHIUSO

THERE ARE SOME FOREIGN WORDS YOU WILL HAVE TO LEARN, LIKE GESCHLOSSEN, FERMÉ, CHIUSO, WHICH ALL MEAN CLOSED.

Caution — Crossways — Ski lift crossing — S.O.S Telephone — First-aid post

Steeper slope — Run narrows — Bumps & hollows — Run crosses road traffic — Through gangway

Turn — Junction — Change of direction — Piste or run marker

THESE ARE SOME OF THE INTERNATIONAL SKI RUN SIGNS YOU ARE LIKELY TO SEE.

IF A FACILITY IS CLOSED, IT IS FOR A REASON. OBEY THE SIGNS.

The ski-way code

IT IS JUST AS IMPORTANT TO OBSERVE THE SKI-WAY CODE ON THE SLOPES AS IT IS TO OBSERVE THE HIGHWAY CODE ON THE ROAD.

DON'T ATTEMPT DARE-DEVIL FEATS BEYOND YOUR ABILITY. SKI WITHIN THE LIMITS OF YOUR SKILL.

WHEN YOU OVERTAKE SLOWER SKIERS, PASS UPHILL OF THEM, AS WIDE AS POSSIBLE.

THE SLOWER SKIER ALWAYS HAS RIGHT OF WAY.

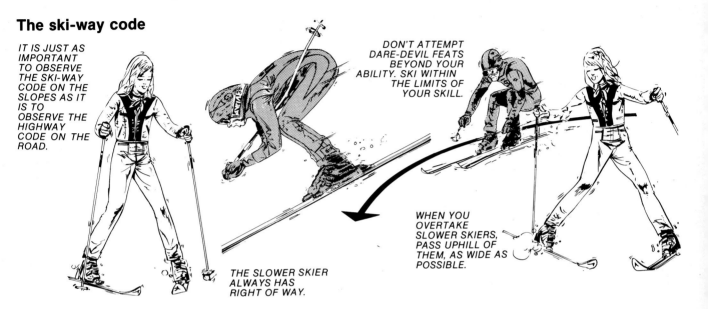

Manners and the skier

KEEP CLEAR OF SKI CLASSES.

NEVER WALK ON A PISTE, AS THE FOOT PRINTS CONSTITUTE A DANGER TO OTHER SKIERS.

WILD AND RECKLESS SKIING IS DANGEROUS TO YOURSELF AND OTHERS, ESPECIALLY THOSE WHO ARE NOT GOOD ENOUGH TO AVOID TROUBLE.

IF YOU SHOULD STOP OR FALL, MOVE OFF THE PISTE QUICKLY. LOOK UPHILL BEFORE MOVING.

Snow conditions

Snow conditions are never constant. They vary according to the time of day, according to which way a slope faces, according to altitude and of course according to the weather and the season. You will find it easier to deal with the variety of conditions you may meet if you can recognise the commoner classifications.

TYPE OF SNOW	CHARACTERISTICS	CAUSES	SKIING QUALITIES
PISTE	A pathway or route of compressed snow.	either by many skiers following the same route or caterpillar tracked piste machine.	Excellent for all skiers, especially when the air is cold and dry.
POWDER	Consists of very small ice crystals. Blows about like dust. Will not form snowballs.	Fresh snow falling in very dry air, without wind at temperatures well below zero.	Excellent surface when lying up to 2ins deep on piste. Exciting challenge to experts when over 9ins deep.
WET HEAVY SNOW (porridge or mashed potato)	Damp to touch, makes snowballs easily. Sticks to and clogs ski boots.	either when snow falls in damp air at around zero or when the temperature and humidity rise after a powder snow fall.	Mediocre if surface only is porridge, but if complete snow cover is wet, very difficult and very dangerous to fall into.
CRUST (sun)	Shiny, roughened surface	Snow cover has been melted and then refrozen.	Breakable Crust which will not carry the skier's weight is difficult and dangerous.
CRUST (wind)	Dull, satin and surface; often lies in slabs which sound hollow when tapped.	When wind blows falling snow into lee drifts and compacts it.	Unbreakable Crust which will easily support the skier is quite difficult to ski on, but not otherwise dangerous.
SPRING OR CORN SNOW	Looks like very large crystals.	Caused by the repeated melting and freezing of the snow cover.	Pleasant to ski when soft and not too deep, but difficult when either frozen solid in the early morning, or when in deep patches of sugar snow in between moguls.
ICE	Smooth and solid glass-like surface.	The rapid freezing of very wet snow.	Very uncomfortable to ski on as it afford very little control. Causes falls and bruising, but seldom broken limbs as skis do not stick to the surface during a fall.
TRAMLINES	Old ski tracks which have frozen solid.	Occurs often in late spring when afternoon tracks in soft snow freeze overnight.	Can be dangerous if skis become wedged in them; otherwise uncomfortable. Ski over them at right angles.
THIN SNOW	Grass, roots or rocks can be seen through the snow surface.	either very slight snow-fall or sudden melting of existing snow cover.	Annoying to ski on as choice of descents limited, and difficult as objects just under the surface catch the soles of the skis, causing damage.

NOTE   Skiers should learn to recognise the boundary between piste and off-piste snow, and remain on the piste unless taken off piste by a guide or ski teacher.

Choosing a resort

When you are deciding which ski resort to go to, try to make an objective analysis of your requirements and relate them carefully to the resort descriptions offered in the brochures.

Which country?

Most British skiers look to the Alps for their skiing, but these days there are all sorts of other possibilities. Eastern Europe has some interesting new ski fields, facilities in Scotland are improving, and now that trans-Atlantic travel has become cheaper it is possible to consider some of the maginificent ski areas in North America. One important factor in choosing a country is the relative value of its currency. You may find that if you choose a resort in Switzerland, for instance, you will have to pay more simply because the Swiss Franc is so expensive.

Which season?

You may not have any choice about when you go, especially if you are still at school. But certain periods, like New Year and Easter are more expensive. You can save money by going low-season, with the added advantage that the snow is often at its best in late January, February and early March, when there will be fewer people, except for during the popular half term school dates and Mardi Gras in France.

Which resort?

There are three kinds of resort. **The old village** is the kind of resort usually found in the traditional ski areas. Old villages have lots of charm and atmosphere, but because they were built long before the days of mass ski holidays, facilities may not be integrated and may even be a bus ride from one another. Some of the lower villages may have a shorter season.

The purpose-built resort usually has all its facilities conveniently close together and co-ordinated with uphill transport. However they can be expensive and somewhat clinically modern.

The ski station is usually nothing more than a few buildings clustered round a cable car station, giving access to a ski area above. Good for day skiing, but they can be too isolated for long stays.

One further consideration: the distance between the resort and the airport. A long bus transfer can mean lost skiing time.

Snow record. Altitude, weather patterns and geographical position all affect the amount of snow a resort receives.

Check the skiing range, that is the height difference between the bottom and the top of the ski slopes.

Check the length of the season on the lower and upper slopes. For instance the lower slopes may have a season from mid December to late April and the upper slopes from early December to late May. Official Tourist Office statistics about the length of the season are only a guide and no one can guarantee snow, especially at the beginning of the season.

Also notice which way ski slopes face — north facing slopes will keep their snow cover longer.

On the piste map on pages 42-43 you will find more details to help you analyse the facilities resorts offer.

Which hotel?

Accommodation: Quality and standards of hotel differ from one country to another. Apart from the obvious considerations of comfort and cuisine (although most young people go to ski, and prefer good sport to good cooking, if they can't have both), the most important factor is the position of your hotel. Is it near the nursery slopes, near the cable car station, and can you ski home at night? In some cases you will have to take a ski bus from the hotel to the lifts and you should discover if this is free or not.

Meals: Normally you will return to your hotel for lunch. If you are a vigorous skier you may well not want to eat a large lunch and may prefer to ask the hotel, the previous day, for a packed lunch, which you can eat in one of the restaurants or cafés on the ski slopes.

Evening Entertainment: Most ski resorts offer lively evening entertainment, usually organised by the representative of the tour company.

If you still have energy left after a day's skiing, most resorts offer toboganning, ice skating and curling (bowling on ice). In the Austrian Tyrol, Switzerland and sometimes in Italy, there are often good folk evenings. Discos are as popular as ever, but watch out for the prices — even a soft drink can prove an expensive luxury.

Reading a piste map

A good piste map tells you a great deal about a resort. The map in the holiday brochure will give you a good deal of information, but you may wish to obtain a more detailed plan from the National Tourist Office of the country concerned. Here are some of the things you can tell from the map.

Ski lifts The plan of the lift system indicates the extent and variety of skiing available in the resort. A good system gives a variety of skiing to all grades of skiers. However, if you are just beginning, don't worry if your resort doesn't have much in the way of black, advanced runs, for experts. Make sure that the resort you choose does have a good variety of skiing at your standard.

Large nursery slopes near the village are an advantage to every one. They allow beginners to ski close to hotels and restaurants, and they help avoid lift queues, as only the better skiers go up the mountain.

There should be a variety of access points to the mountain — several lifts out of the village, so that no one lift becomes too crowded.

The lifts should provide as many linking runs as possible, so that you can reach almost any ski area by several different means.

Avoid bottlenecks A bad system creates bottlenecks. If there is only one lift, linking the village and the main ski area, there may be queues every morning, and at night also, if there is not enough snow in the village and everyone has to go up the mountain to ski. The lift layout will also show you how near the lift stations are to the village.

Season A good piste map may indicate the length of the season on the lower and upper slopes.

Standard of skiing Most European centres use a colour code to classify ski runs. Nursery slopes are often coloured *green* on the piste map. *Blue* runs are for those who have managed snowplough turns, usually after about a week's skiing. *Red* slopes are for intermediate skiers, while *black* slopes are steep and difficult enough to challenge advanced skiers.

Range of skiing If the village is at 1330m (4,250 ft.) and the top of the highest lift is 3,220m (10,500 ft.), for example, the range of skiing is likely to be quite extensive. A smaller range can mean shorter runs and less varied skiing.

North and south facing slopes North facing slopes keep their snow longer, but obviously it's more pleasant to ski in the sun. A village that provides slopes facing in more than one direction has an advantage — a choice of good snow and or good sun.

This map shows two imaginary ski resorts. On it you will find many of the points to look for when choosing where to ski – altitude, lift systems, variety of runs. The villages on the map are not based on any real places, but they do illustrate some of the better and less good facilities you will find offered at many resorts.

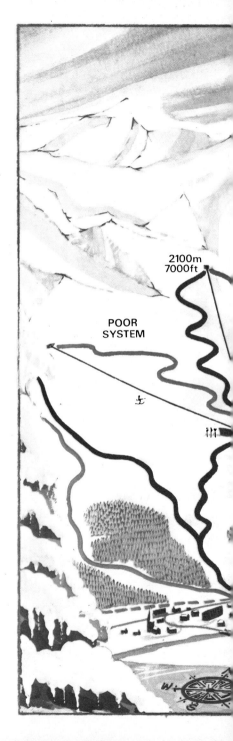

2100m
7000ft

POOR
SYSTEM

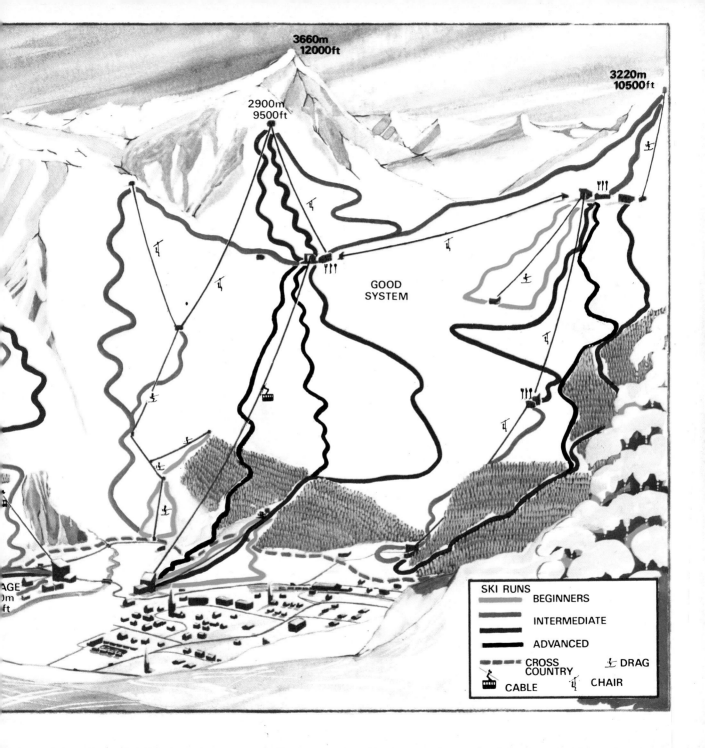

3660m
12000ft

3220m
10500ft

2900m
9500ft

GOOD
SYSTEM

AGE
0m
ft

SKI RUNS	
BEGINNERS	
INTERMEDIATE	
ADVANCED	
CROSS COUNTRY	DRAG
CABLE	CHAIR

Danger on the slopes

Accidents can happen in skiing, but there is no need to be put off by the dangers. It is best to prevent problems, by knowing what to do. Know where to find the ski patrol, who are responsible for policing the slopes. They can usually be contacted at the cable car station, or through lift attendants, who usually have telephones.

The rogue ski

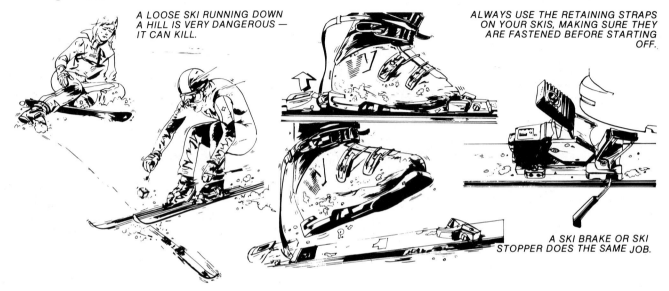

A LOOSE SKI RUNNING DOWN A HILL IS VERY DANGEROUS — IT CAN KILL.

ALWAYS USE THE RETAINING STRAPS ON YOUR SKIS, MAKING SURE THEY ARE FASTENED BEFORE STARTING OFF.

A SKI BRAKE OR SKI STOPPER DOES THE SAME JOB.

Getting lost

IN POOR VISIBILITY KEEP TO FAMILIAR RUNS: KEEP AN EYE ON THE MARKER POSTS: KEEP WITHIN EARSHOT OF LIFTS; NEVER SKI ALONE.

IN FOG OR WHITEOUT DON'T VENTURE OUT ONTO THE MOUNTAIN. IF YOU ARE SKIING ALREADY, HEAD FOR A SAFE POINT, LIKE A LIFT STATION.

WHATEVER HAPPENS DO NOT SKI OR WALK STRAIGHT DOWNHILL. YOU COULD EASILY DROP STRAIGHT OFF A CLIFF, OR DOWN A STEEP SLOPE.

THE INTERNATIONAL MOUNTAIN DISTRESS SIGNAL IS SIX REGULAR SHOUTS, WHISTLES, OR FLASHES OF LIGHT IN A MINUTE. THE ANSWER IS THREE RESPONSES A MINUTE, WITH ONE MINUTE INTERVAL BEFORE THE NEXT RESPONSE.

Accident procedure

IF YOU ENCOUNTER AN ACCIDENT, STOP AND ASSIST IF REQUIRED.

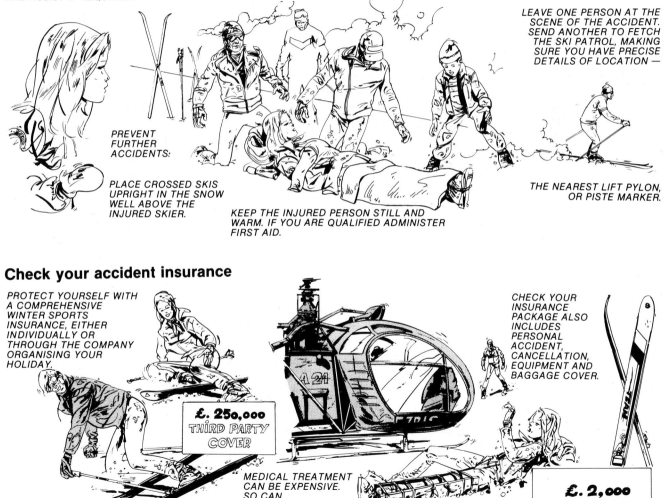

LEAVE ONE PERSON AT THE SCENE OF THE ACCIDENT. SEND ANOTHER TO FETCH THE SKI PATROL, MAKING SURE YOU HAVE PRECISE DETAILS OF LOCATION —

PREVENT FURTHER ACCIDENTS:

PLACE CROSSED SKIS UPRIGHT IN THE SNOW WELL ABOVE THE INJURED SKIER.

KEEP THE INJURED PERSON STILL AND WARM. IF YOU ARE QUALIFIED ADMINISTER FIRST AID.

THE NEAREST LIFT PYLON, OR PISTE MARKER.

Check your accident insurance

PROTECT YOURSELF WITH A COMPREHENSIVE WINTER SPORTS INSURANCE, EITHER INDIVIDUALLY OR THROUGH THE COMPANY ORGANISING YOUR HOLIDAY.

CHECK YOUR INSURANCE PACKAGE ALSO INCLUDES PERSONAL ACCIDENT, CANCELLATION, EQUIPMENT AND BAGGAGE COVER.

£. 250,000
THIRD PARTY
COVER

£. 2,000
MEDICAL AND
EMERGENCY
COVER

YOU NEED THIRD PARTY LIABILITY COVER AS YOU COULD BE HELD LIABLE FOR ANY DAMAGE CAUSED TO SOMEONE ELSE EVEN THOUGH SKIING IS CLASSED AS A HAZARDOUS SPORT.

MEDICAL TREATMENT CAN BE EXPENSIVE. SO CAN TRANSPORTATION OF AN INJURED SKIER FROM THE ACCIDENT SCENE — POSSIBLY BY HELICOPTER.

LEARNING TO SKI

There are many different ways of learning to ski. The Austrian, Italian, French and Swiss Ski Schools all have their own teaching methods. Some of them stress different aspects of skiing at different moments in the process of learning. And all of them tend to think that their way is the only correct way. So, it is important to remember that they are all aiming at the same objective — enabling you to descend the mountain with control and safety, using a variety of techniques according to snow conditions, terrain and your level of ability. If you can do that, you will develop confidence on skis and enjoy your holiday. The techniques outlined here are common to all teaching systems. You will gain most from your ski school instructor if you relate his teaching to the advice given in this book.

A child is guided through poles to learn ski control.

Warm up your muscles

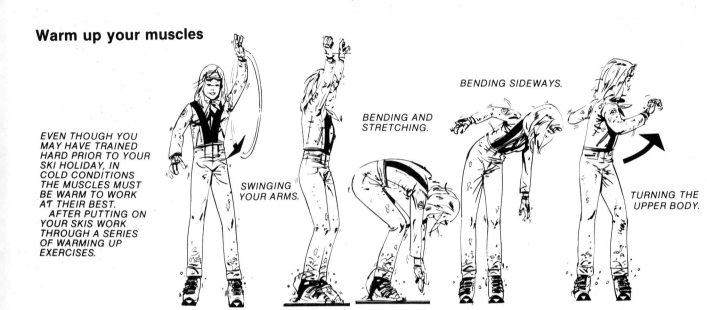

EVEN THOUGH YOU
MAY HAVE TRAINED
HARD PRIOR TO YOUR
SKI HOLIDAY, IN
COLD CONDITIONS
THE MUSCLES MUST
BE WARM TO WORK
AT THEIR BEST.
AFTER PUTTING ON
YOUR SKIS WORK
THROUGH A SERIES
OF WARMING UP
EXERCISES.

SWINGING
YOUR ARMS.

BENDING AND
STRETCHING.

BENDING SIDEWAYS.

TURNING THE
UPPER BODY.

Putting on skis on the flat

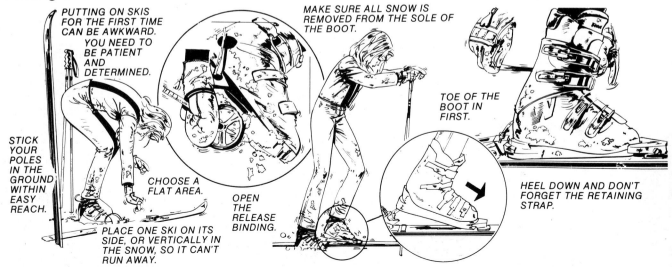

PUTTING ON SKIS
FOR THE FIRST TIME
CAN BE AWKWARD.
YOU NEED TO
BE PATIENT
AND
DETERMINED.

MAKE SURE ALL SNOW IS
REMOVED FROM THE SOLE OF
THE BOOT.

STICK
YOUR
POLES
IN THE
GROUND
WITHIN
EASY
REACH.

CHOOSE A
FLAT AREA.

OPEN
THE
RELEASE
BINDING.

PLACE ONE SKI ON ITS
SIDE, OR VERTICALLY IN
THE SNOW, SO IT CAN'T
RUN AWAY.

TOE OF THE
BOOT IN
FIRST.

HEEL DOWN AND DON'T
FORGET THE RETAINING
STRAP.

Putting on skis on a slope

TO START WITH YOU WON'T OFTEN BE EXPECTED TO PUT ON YOUR SKIS WHILE STANDING ON A SLOPE.

BUT IF AND WHEN YOU HAVE TO DO SO, START BY POSITIONING YOURSELF AND YOUR SKIS AT RIGHT ANGLES TO THE SLOPE.

KEEP THE EDGES OF THE SKIS INTO THE HILL.

PLACE THE POLES AND ONE SKI IN THE SNOW ON YOUR UPHILL SIDE.

PUT THE UPHILL SKI ON FIRST.

TURN ROUND SO THAT THE OTHER FOOT IS NOW UPHILL AND PUT ON THE SECOND SKI.

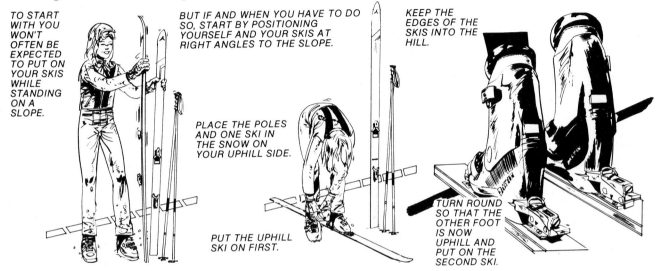

Ski familiarisation

FEEL THE WEIGHT AND SIZE OF YOUR SKIS.

PRESS THE SKIS ONTO THEIR SIDES IN EACH DIRECTION.

ROCK FORWARDS AND BACKWARDS TO FEEL THE SUPPORT THE BOOTS GIVE.

BEND YOUR KNEE AND LIFT THE HEEL OF EACH SKI IN TURN...

...NOW LIFT THE TIPS.

LIFT THE WHOLE SKI UP KEEPING IT LEVEL.

TAP THE TIP OF ONE SKI EITHER SIDE OF THE OTHER.

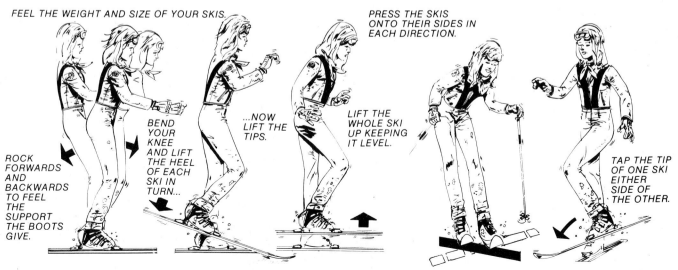

How to stand on skis

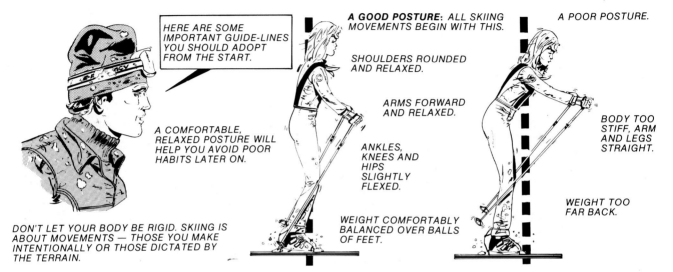

HERE ARE SOME IMPORTANT GUIDE-LINES YOU SHOULD ADOPT FROM THE START.

A COMFORTABLE, RELAXED POSTURE WILL HELP YOU AVOID POOR HABITS LATER ON.

DON'T LET YOUR BODY BE RIGID. SKIING IS ABOUT MOVEMENTS — THOSE YOU MAKE INTENTIONALLY OR THOSE DICTATED BY THE TERRAIN.

A GOOD POSTURE: ALL SKIING MOVEMENTS BEGIN WITH THIS.

SHOULDERS ROUNDED AND RELAXED.

ARMS FORWARD AND RELAXED.

ANKLES, KNEES AND HIPS SLIGHTLY FLEXED.

WEIGHT COMFORTABLY BALANCED OVER BALLS OF FEET.

A POOR POSTURE.

BODY TOO STIFF, ARM AND LEGS STRAIGHT.

WEIGHT TOO FAR BACK.

Walking on skis

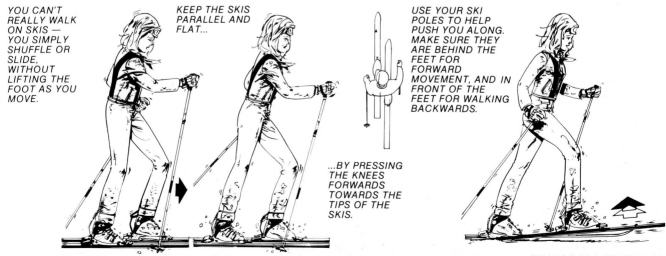

YOU CAN'T REALLY WALK ON SKIS — YOU SIMPLY SHUFFLE OR SLIDE, WITHOUT LIFTING THE FOOT AS YOU MOVE.

KEEP THE SKIS PARALLEL AND FLAT...

...BY PRESSING THE KNEES FORWARDS TOWARDS THE TIPS OF THE SKIS.

USE YOUR SKI POLES TO HELP PUSH YOU ALONG. MAKE SURE THEY ARE BEHIND THE FEET FOR FORWARD MOVEMENT, AND IN FRONT OF THE FEET FOR WALKING BACKWARDS.

TRY NOT TO LIFT YOUR SKIS.

Changing direction—the clock turn

NOW YOU'VE LEARNED TO WALK, HERE'S HOW TO CHANGE DIRECTION. IMAGINE YOUR SKIS AS THE HANDS OF A CLOCK.

WITH A SIMILAR MOVEMENT BRING THE OTHER SKI ALONGSIDE. REPEAT.

THE SAME MANOEUVRE CAN BE PRACTISED BY PIVOTING ON THE TAILS.

START WITH THE SKIS TOGETHER.

PIVOTING THE LEFT SKI ON ITS TIP, STEP OUT IN A V-SHAPE.

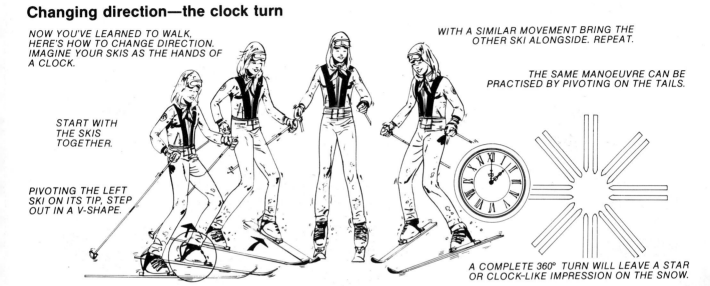

A COMPLETE 360° TURN WILL LEAVE A STAR OR CLOCK-LIKE IMPRESSION ON THE SNOW.

Learning to skate

SKATING WILL HELP YOU INCREASE SPEED ON THE FLAT OR GIVE YOU THE IMPETUS TO GO UP A SLIGHT SLOPE.

FROM A STARTING POSITION WITH SKIS PARALLEL, LIFT ONE SKI AND POINT THE TIP OUTWARDS.

THE MOVEMENT IS CONTINUOUS — PUSHING OFF ONE SKI, ON TO THE OTHER.

REMEMBER TO KEEP YOUR STICKS OUTSIDE YOUR SKIS — OR YOU WILL TRIP YOURSELF UP.

PUSH OFF BY PRESSING AGAINST THE INSIDE EDGE OF THE SKI.

AS YOU SKATE ONTO THE SLIDING SKI TRY TO KEEP YOUR HEAD OVER YOUR FOOT.

Stepping up a slope

WHEN YOU ARE CONFIDENT ON THE FLAT, IT'S TIME TO CLIMB THE HILL.
THE STEEPEST LINE DOWN A SLOPE IS CALLED THE FALL LINE. IF A BALL WAS DROPPED DOWN A SLOPE IT WOULD ROLL DOWN THE FALL LINE — THE FASTEST DIRECT LINE DOWN THE HILL.

START OFF WITH YOUR SKIS AT RIGHT ANGLES TO THE FALL LINE.

THE FALL LINE.

SET YOUR SKIS ON THEIR UPHILL EDGES BY GENTLY PRESSING KNEES AND HIPS UPHILL. STANDING ON THE BIG TOE OF THE LOWER FOOT AND THE LITTLE TOE OF THE UPPER FOOT. IF YOUR SKIS ARE TOO FLAT, THEY WILL SLIP DOWNHILL.

KEEP THE SKIS PARALLEL.

ANKLES BENT FORWARDS.

SKIS SLIGHTLY APART, UPPER FOOT FORWARD.

The herringbone

THE NEXT STEP IS THE HERRINGBONE.

FACE UPHILL IN THE FALL LINE MAKING A V-SHAPE WITH YOUR SKIS.

BEND YOUR KNEES AND PRESS THEM INWARDS TO GRIP WITH THE INSIDE EDGES.

ADVANCE ONE SKI AT A TIME USING YOUR SKI STICKS TO HELP YOU.

CHANGE THE GRIP ON YOUR SKI STICKS AND PLACE THEM BEHIND YOU.

CHANGE TO A SIDESTEP IF THE SLOPE GETS STEEPER.

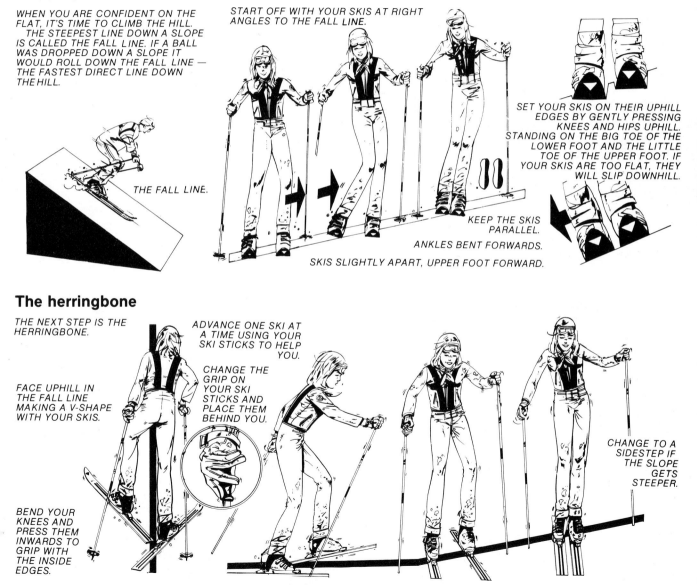

The first run

Everyone falls when they begin. But some people find it harder to balance than others. If you keep falling it may help to widen your ski base and lower your centre of gravity by crouching. It's not graceful, but it will help you balance! And then you can progress with the techniques shown here.

Turning on the slope

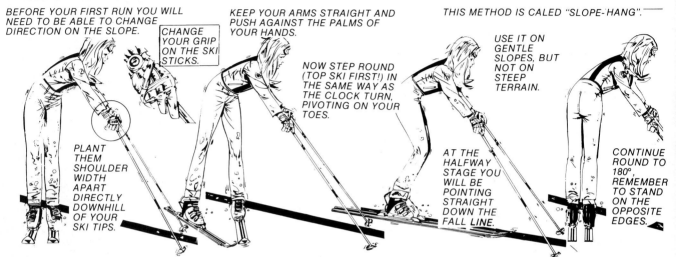

BEFORE YOUR FIRST RUN YOU WILL NEED TO BE ABLE TO CHANGE DIRECTION ON THE SLOPE.

CHANGE YOUR GRIP ON THE SKI STICKS.

PLANT THEM SHOULDER WIDTH APART DIRECTLY DOWNHILL OF YOUR SKI TIPS.

KEEP YOUR ARMS STRAIGHT AND PUSH AGAINST THE PALMS OF YOUR HANDS.

NOW STEP ROUND (TOP SKI FIRST!) IN THE SAME WAY AS THE CLOCK TURN, PIVOTING ON YOUR TOES.

AT THE HALFWAY STAGE YOU WILL BE POINTING STRAIGHT DOWN THE FALL LINE.

THIS METHOD IS CALED "SLOPE-HANG".

USE IT ON GENTLE SLOPES, BUT NOT ON STEEP TERRAIN.

CONTINUE ROUND TO 180°, REMEMBER TO STAND ON THE OPPOSITE EDGES.

Straight running

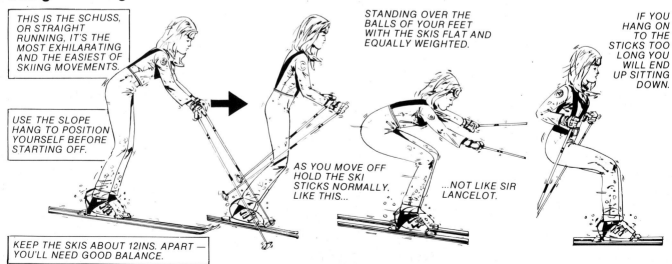

THIS IS THE SCHUSS, OR STRAIGHT RUNNING. IT'S THE MOST EXHILARATING AND THE EASIEST OF SKIING MOVEMENTS.

USE THE SLOPE HANG TO POSITION YOURSELF BEFORE STARTING OFF.

KEEP THE SKIS ABOUT 12INS. APART — YOU'LL NEED GOOD BALANCE.

STANDING OVER THE BALLS OF YOUR FEET WITH THE SKIS FLAT AND EQUALLY WEIGHTED.

AS YOU MOVE OFF HOLD THE SKI STICKS NORMALLY. LIKE THIS...

...NOT LIKE SIR LANCELOT.

IF YOU HANG ON TO THE STICKS TOO LONG YOU WILL END UP SITTING DOWN.

Develop your balance

GOOD BALANCE IS ESSENTIAL FOR RELAXED POSTURE.

TO IMPROVE YOUR BALANCE TRY SOME EXERCISES WHILE RUNNING STRAIGHT.

CROUCH DOWN, TRY TO TOUCH YOUR TOES...

ROCKING — FORWARDS AND BACKWARDS FEEL FOR SUPPORT ON THE FRONTS AND BACKS OF YOUR BOOTS.

ON THE WAY DOWN TRY PICKING UP OBJECTS FROM THE GROUND — USE A GLOVE OR A HAT.

WIDE BASE — MORE STABILITY

...AND STRETCH HIGH. ALWAYS REMEMBER TO MAKE SURE THAT YOU ARE STANDING OVER THE BALLS OF YOUR FEET.

SKIERS WHO HAVE DIFFICULTIES STAYING UPRIGHT, NEED TO CROUCH, AND OPEN THE SKIS, SLIGHTLY, FOR A WIDER BASE.

Learn to fall correctly

ALL SKIERS FALL — EVEN EXPERTS. IF YOU LEARN HOW TO FALL PROPERLY YOU CAN AVOID INJURY.

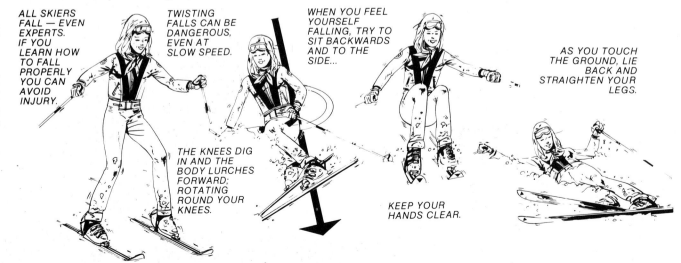

TWISTING FALLS CAN BE DANGEROUS, EVEN AT SLOW SPEED.

WHEN YOU FEEL YOURSELF FALLING, TRY TO SIT BACKWARDS AND TO THE SIDE...

AS YOU TOUCH THE GROUND, LIE BACK AND STRAIGHTEN YOUR LEGS.

THE KNEES DIG IN AND THE BODY LURCHES FORWARD; ROTATING ROUND YOUR KNEES.

KEEP YOUR HANDS CLEAR.

Getting up after a fall

BEFORE YOU TRY TO STAND UP, POSITION YOUR SKIS BELOW YOU AND ACROSS THE FALL LINE.

WITH YOUR HAND ON THE GROUND NEAR YOUR UPHILL THIGH, PUSH UP MOVING YOUR WEIGHT OVER ONTO YOUR FEET.

IN SOFT SNOW PUSH YOURSELF UP OFF YOUR SKI STICKS LAID FLAT OR CROSSED IN THE SNOW.

GETTING UP AFTER A FALL CAN BE A TIRESOME BUSINESS — ESPECIALLY IF YOU HAVE HAD THE WIND KNOCKED OUT OF YOU.

SIT AS CLOSE TO YOUR FEET AS YOU CAN WITH YOUR UPPER BODY BENT FORWARD OVER THE FRONT OF THE SKIS.

The gliding snowplough

SNOWPLOUGHING IS THE EASIEST MEANS OF CONTROLLING YOUR SKIS ON A GENTLE SLOPE. WITH YOUR SKIS IN A V-SHAPE, GLIDE DOWN THE FALL LINE. KEEP EQUAL WEIGHT ON BOTH SKIS.

HOLD THE SKIS IN THE PLOUGH SHAPE MAINTAINING EQUAL PRESSURE AS YOU GLIDE DOWN THE SLOPE.

IMPROVE YOUR SNOWPLOUGH GLIDE WITH A BRUSHING ACTION.
LET YOUR SKIS RUN INTO A NARROW V THEN SINK DOWN TO PUSH OUT AGAIN INTO THE ORIGINAL PLOUGH.

THE SKIS SKID AGAINST THEIR INNER EDGES.

TRY GLIDING IN A LOW CROUCH, AND THEN STRAIGHTENING UP — ALL WITHOUT ALTERING THE ANGLE OF THE PLOUGH.

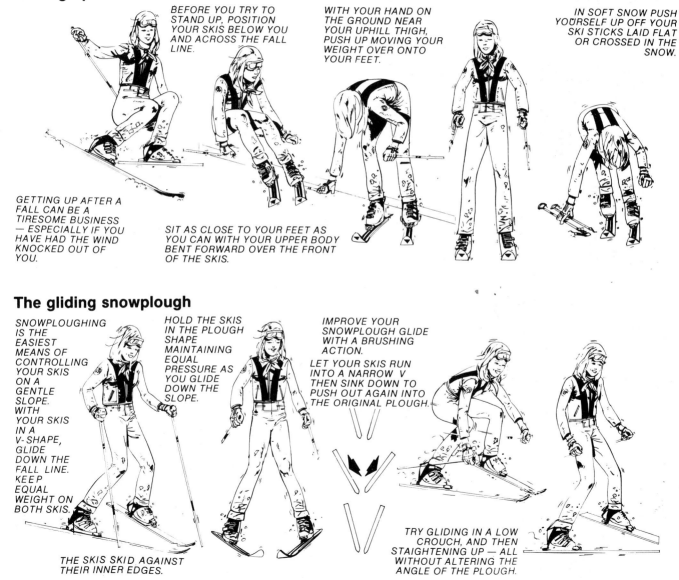

For small children learning to ski through play is an effective method.

Snowplough braking

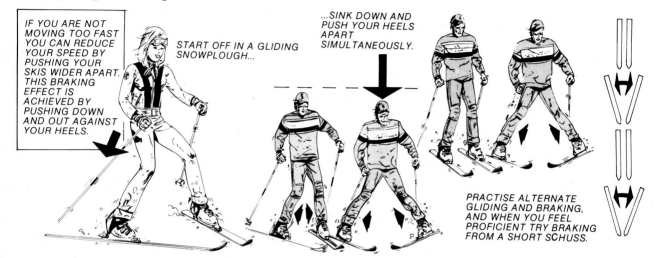

IF YOU ARE NOT MOVING TOO FAST YOU CAN REDUCE YOUR SPEED BY PUSHING YOUR SKIS WIDER APART. THIS BRAKING EFFECT IS ACHIEVED BY PUSHING DOWN AND OUT AGAINST YOUR HEELS.

START OFF IN A GLIDING SNOWPLOUGH...

...SINK DOWN AND PUSH YOUR HEELS APART SIMULTANEOUSLY.

PRACTISE ALTERNATE GLIDING AND BRAKING, AND WHEN YOU FEEL PROFICIENT TRY BRAKING FROM A SHORT SCHUSS.

The first turn

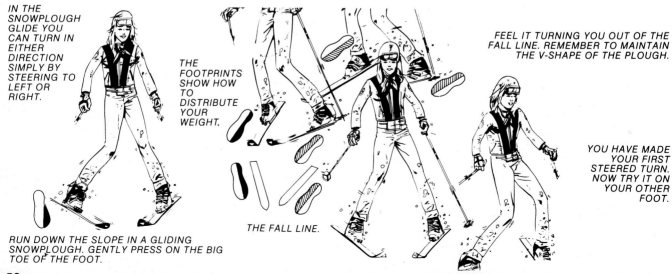

IN THE SNOWPLOUGH GLIDE YOU CAN TURN IN EITHER DIRECTION SIMPLY BY STEERING TO LEFT OR RIGHT.

THE FOOTPRINTS SHOW HOW TO DISTRIBUTE YOUR WEIGHT.

FEEL IT TURNING YOU OUT OF THE FALL LINE. REMEMBER TO MAINTAIN THE V-SHAPE OF THE PLOUGH.

YOU HAVE MADE YOUR FIRST STEERED TURN. NOW TRY IT ON YOUR OTHER FOOT.

THE FALL LINE.

RUN DOWN THE SLOPE IN A GLIDING SNOWPLOUGH. GENTLY PRESS ON THE BIG TOE OF THE FOOT.

Feeling for the resistance

THE BEST WAY TO LEARN TO SKI IS BY "FEEL".

FEEL FOR THE RESISTANCE UNDER YOUR SKIS...

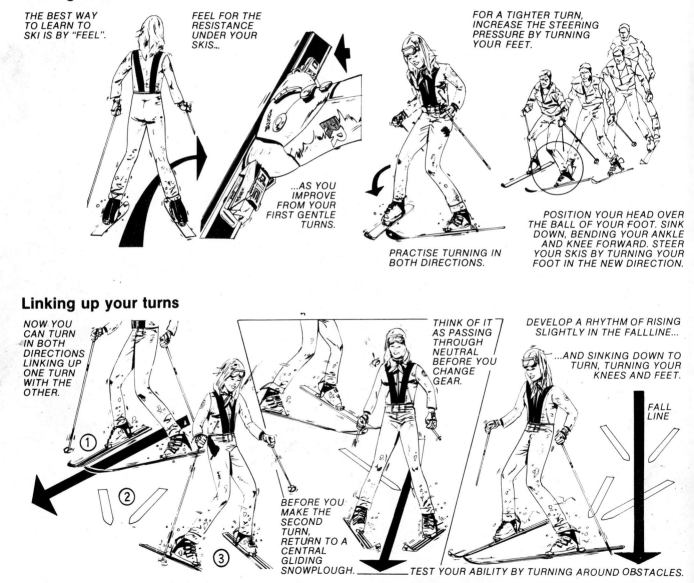

...AS YOU IMPROVE FROM YOUR FIRST GENTLE TURNS.

PRACTISE TURNING IN BOTH DIRECTIONS.

FOR A TIGHTER TURN, INCREASE THE STEERING PRESSURE BY TURNING YOUR FEET.

POSITION YOUR HEAD OVER THE BALL OF YOUR FOOT. SINK DOWN, BENDING YOUR ANKLE AND KNEE FORWARD. STEER YOUR SKIS BY TURNING YOUR FOOT IN THE NEW DIRECTION.

Linking up your turns

NOW YOU CAN TURN IN BOTH DIRECTIONS LINKING UP ONE TURN WITH THE OTHER.

THINK OF IT AS PASSING THROUGH NEUTRAL BEFORE YOU CHANGE GEAR.

DEVELOP A RHYTHM OF RISING SLIGHTLY IN THE FALLLINE...

...AND SINKING DOWN TO TURN, TURNING YOUR KNEES AND FEET.

FALL LINE

BEFORE YOU MAKE THE SECOND TURN, RETURN TO A CENTRAL GLIDING SNOWPLOUGH.

TEST YOUR ABILITY BY TURNING AROUND OBSTACLES.

MORE ADVANCED SKIING

The aim of most skiers is to ski parallel. While you were on easy, shallow slopes, you could use basic techniques, like the snowplough, to steer, slow down or stop. Naturally when you progress and travel faster you will need to develop your technique to cope with speed and steeper terrain. If you gradually reduce the angle of your plough you can bring your skis almost parallel, if still a little apart. This enables one ski to reinforce the work of the other. And it cuts down the time and effort required to turn — although it requires more sensitive balance.

This is called parallel skiing. When you feel at home with this method you are no longer a beginner, you are on the way to becoming an expert.

A multiple exposure showing the sequence of movements in a turn.

Skiing across the slope

TRAVERSING MEANS GOING ACROSS THE SLOPE, BUT SPECIFICALLY WITHOUT ANY SIDEWAYS MOVEMENT.

THE STEEPER THE SLOPE — THE MORE "ANGULATION".

8INS (20CMS)

POSITION YOUR SKIS ABOUT 8INS (20CMS) APART WITH THE TOP SKI SLIGHTLY FORWARD.

SET THE SKIS ON THEIR EDGES. MOST OF YOUR WEIGHT SHOULD BE ON THE LOWER SKI.

WHEN TRAVERSING YOU MUST HOLD A LINE ACROSS A SLOPE...

...BY TRACKING ON THE SKI EDGES, WITH NO SIDEWAYS MOVEMENT. .

"ANGULATE" YOUR BODY — HEAD OVER THE LOWER FOOT.

Slipping down the hill

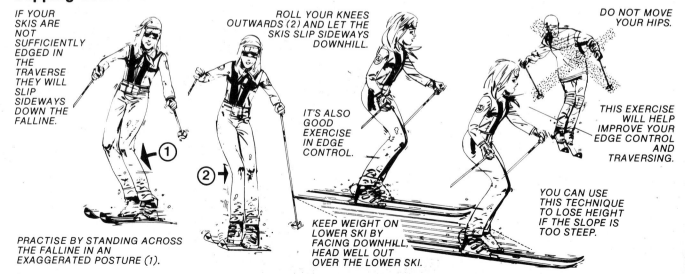

IF YOUR SKIS ARE NOT SUFFICIENTLY EDGED IN THE TRAVERSE THEY WILL SLIP SIDEWAYS DOWN THE FALLINE.

ROLL YOUR KNEES OUTWARDS (2) AND LET THE SKIS SLIP SIDEWAYS DOWNHILL.

DO NOT MOVE YOUR HIPS.

IT'S ALSO GOOD EXERCISE IN EDGE CONTROL.

THIS EXERCISE WILL HELP IMPROVE YOUR EDGE CONTROL AND TRAVERSING.

PRACTISE BY STANDING ACROSS THE FALLINE IN AN EXAGGERATED POSTURE (1).

KEEP WEIGHT ON LOWER SKI BY FACING DOWNHILL, HEAD WELL OUT OVER THE LOWER SKI.

YOU CAN USE THIS TECHNIQUE TO LOSE HEIGHT IF THE SLOPE IS TOO STEEP.

Learn to skid your skis

SKIDDING (NOT SLIPPING) IS AN IMPORTANT PART OF TURNING.

IN A GLIDING SNOWPLOUGH YOU CAN FEEL THE SKIS SKIDDING FORWARDS AND SIDEWAYS AGAINST THEIR INSIDE EDGES.

TO START A TURN, QUICKLY LIFT ONE SKI PARALLEL TO THE OTHER.

IF YOU FLATTEN YOUR SKIS YOU WILL SLIP DOWN, SIDEWAYS.

ANGULATE AND KEEP YOUR HEAD OVER THE LOWER SKI.

YOU WILL FIND THAT YOU ARE SKIDDING ON BOTH SKIS, WHILE CHANGING DIRECTION SLIGHTLY.

Learn to skid by shuffling

PRACTISE SKIDDING BY A TAIL SIDE SHUFFLE FROM A STEEP TRAVERSE.

1 FEEL FOR THE BIG TOE OF THE LOWER SKI. PRESS ON IT AND DISPLACE THE TAIL OF THE LOWER SKI.

YOU NEED MOMENTUM, AND THEREFORE A REASONABLE AMOUNT OF SPEED TO SKID.

2 NOW FEEL FOR THE LITTLE TOE OF THE UPPER SKI. PRESS ON IT AND PULL THE UPPER SKI ALONGSIDE.

3 REPEAT IN RAPID SUCCESSION UNTIL YOU FEEL THE SKI SKIDDING FREELY.

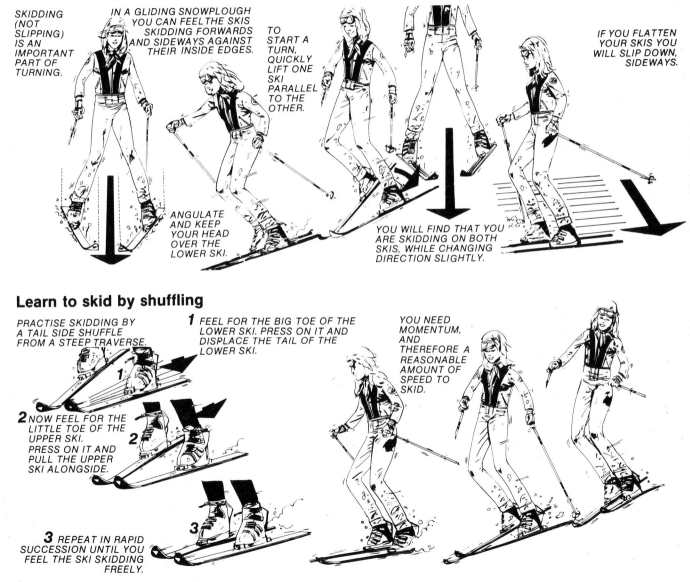

Plough wedeln into parallel —the direct method

YOU CAN DEVELOP PARALLELS BY LINKING UP SHORT SNOWPLOUGH TURNS. YOU NEED STRONG LEG MOVEMENTS AND RHYTHM.

BUILD UP A STRONG RYTHMICAL ACTION, USING ALTERNATE FEET TO STEER. PUT YOUR HEAD OVER THE STEERED SKI.

You need good technique to ski off piste through deep snow, or forest.

PRACTISE ON FAIRLY EVEN TERRAIN. START OFF IN THE FALL LINE MAKING A SERIES OF TURNS.

GRADUALLY NARROW THE PLOUGH UNTIL IT IS COMPLETELY ELIMINATED, BUT KEEP YOUR SKIS ABOUT 8 ins. APART.

CONCENTRATE ON STEERING THE SKIS WITH A STRONG DOWN ACTION. ACCENTUATE THE STRAIGHTENING OF THE LEGS BETWEEN TURNS.

CONTINUE TO WORK YOUR LEGS INDEPENDENTLY, EVEN WHEN YOUR SKIS MOVE CLOSER TOGETHER.

Use your sticks to help you turn

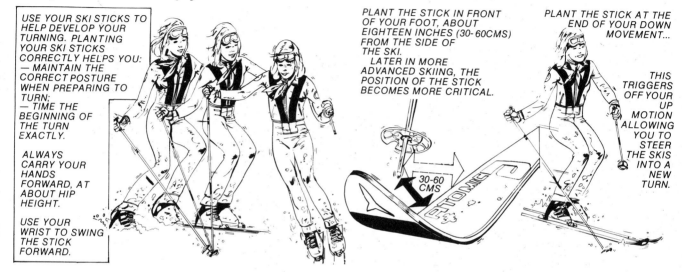

USE YOUR SKI STICKS TO HELP DEVELOP YOUR TURNING. PLANTING YOUR SKI STICKS CORRECTLY HELPS YOU:
— MAINTAIN THE CORRECT POSTURE WHEN PREPARING TO TURN;
— TIME THE BEGINNING OF THE TURN EXACTLY.

ALWAYS CARRY YOUR HANDS FORWARD, AT ABOUT HIP HEIGHT.

USE YOUR WRIST TO SWING THE STICK FORWARD.

PLANT THE STICK IN FRONT OF YOUR FOOT, ABOUT EIGHTEEN INCHES (30-60CMS) FROM THE SIDE OF THE SKI.
LATER IN MORE ADVANCED SKIING, THE POSITION OF THE STICK BECOMES MORE CRITICAL.

30-60 CMS

PLANT THE STICK AT THE END OF YOUR DOWN MOVEMENT...

THIS TRIGGERS OFF YOUR UP MOTION ALLOWING YOU TO STEER THE SKIS INTO A NEW TURN.

Closing the inner ski

IN PARALLEL TURNS THE INNER SKI REINFORCES THE DOMINANT OUTER SKI.

TO CHANGE EFFECTIVELY FROM A SNOWPLOUGH TO A TURNING PARALLEL SKID...

...ROLL YOUR INSIDE SKI ONTO ITS OUTER EDGE...

IN SNOWPLOUGHING THE SKIS OPPOSE EACH OTHER WHILST SKIDDING.

...AND SIMULTANEOUSLY DRAW IT PARALLEL TO THE OUTER SKI.

68

Unweighting to help you turn

IN ORDER TO TURN YOU MUST CHANGE THE EDGES OF YOUR SKIS. THIS IS HELPED BY UNWEIGHTING (TAKING THE WEIGHT OFF) THE SKIS.

THE MOST COMMON TECHNIQUE IS CALLED UP-UNWEIGHTING.

IMAGINE YOURSELF ON A PAIR OF SCALES.

FIRST SINK DOWN FLEXING THE LEGS AND HIPS.

THEN EXTEND YOUR BODY RAPIDLY UPWARDS; THE WEIGHT IS EFFECTIVELY DECREASED AT THE HIGHEST POINT.

YOU CHANGE EDGES, TURN, AND GO BACK TO YOUR NORMAL WEIGHT.

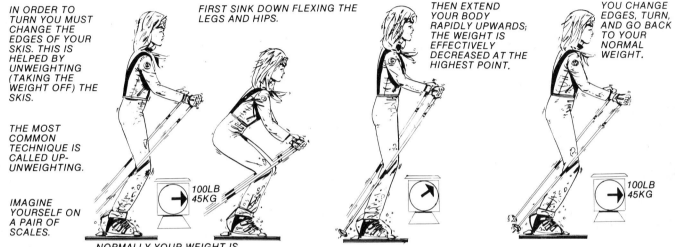

NORMALLY YOUR WEIGHT IS 100LB (45KG), FOR EXAMPLE

100LB 45KG

100LB 45KG

Compression turns

IN SOME COUNTRIES SKI SCHOOLS TEACH WITH THE EMPHASIS ON **DOWN** MOVEMENTS "CROUCHING".

DOWN UNWEIGHTING IS A MUCH FASTER MOVEMENT, WHICH GIVES YOU A QUICKER EDGE CHANGE, USED MOSTLY BY RACERS.

AT THE END OF THE DOWN-MOVEMENT, AN INCREASE IN PRESSURE RESULTS, AS NORMAL CONTACT IS MADE.

A DOWN MOVEMENT WITH STRONG FLEXION OF THE LEGS AND BODY REDUCES EFFECTIVE WEIGHT.

THIS MEANS THAT IN THE SNOWPLOUGH, FOR EXAMPLE, YOU WILL BE TAUGHT TO ADOPT A LOW STANCE IN THE FALL LINE AND TO EXTEND AS YOU TURN. THIS IS OFTEN MISUNDERSTOOD AS DOWN UNWEIGHTING. IN FACT IT IS A PREPARATION FOR COMPRESSION TURNS.

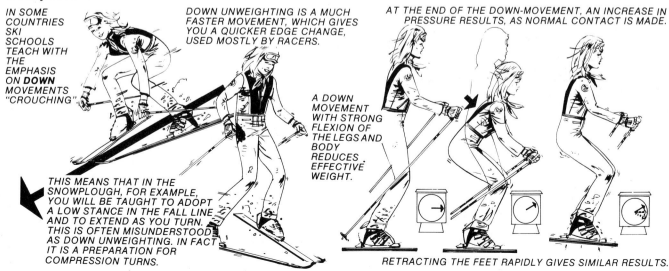

RETRACTING THE FEET RAPIDLY GIVES SIMILAR RESULTS.

69

Hopping

AN EASY WAY TO PARALLEL TURNS IS BY HOPPING. BUILD UP TO IT WITH A SERIES OF EXERCISES.

2 PREPARE TO HOP...

3 HOP UP AND FORWARD.

THE TIPS OF THE SKIS WILL REMAIN ON THE SNOW.

USE YOUR STICKS LIKE THIS.

PLANT THE POLE BESIDE THE TIP OF YOUR SKI, AND USE IT TO TRIGGER THE UP-MOVEMENT

1 *FIRST SKI DOWN THE FALL LINE ON A GENTLE SLOPE, HOPPING UP THE TAILS OF YOUR SKIS.*

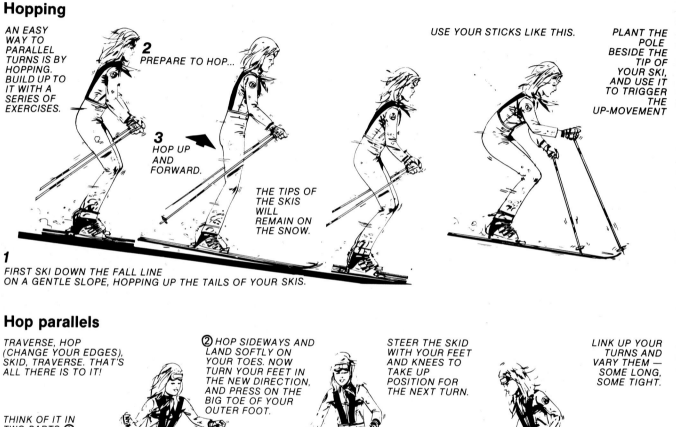

Hop parallels

TRAVERSE, HOP (CHANGE YOUR EDGES), SKID, TRAVERSE. THAT'S ALL THERE IS TO IT!

THINK OF IT IN TWO PARTS ① *PREPARE BY SINKING DOWN AND PLANTING POLE WELL FORWARD.*

② *HOP SIDEWAYS AND LAND SOFTLY ON YOUR TOES. NOW TURN YOUR FEET IN THE NEW DIRECTION, AND PRESS ON THE BIG TOE OF YOUR OUTER FOOT.*

STEER THE SKID WITH YOUR FEET AND KNEES TO TAKE UP POSITION FOR THE NEXT TURN.

LINK UP YOUR TURNS AND VARY THEM — SOME LONG, SOME TIGHT.

Kick turns

AT SOME TIME YOU WILL NEED TO TURN AROUND ON A STEEP SLOPE, AND IN A CONFINED SPACE.

TO DO THIS USE THE KICK TURN.

SWING YOUR LOWER SKI ONTO ITS TAIL.

THEN, BY BENDING YOUR KNEE, SWING THE SKI ROUND PARALLEL AND IN THE OPPOSITE DIRECTION TO THE OTHER ONE.

NOW STAND ON IT AND LIFT THE OTHER SKI ROUND TO BRING IT ALONGSIDE.

KEEP PRESSING AGAINST YOUR STICKS UNTIL YOU HAVE COMPLETED THE TURN.

THE STEEPER THE SLOPE THE MORE YOU NEED TO DIG YOUR EDGES IN.

PLACE YOUR STICKS BEHIND YOU FOR SUPPORT.

Up-unweighting into parallels

REFINE YOUR HOP PARALLELS AND KEEP IN CONTACT WITH THE SNOW.

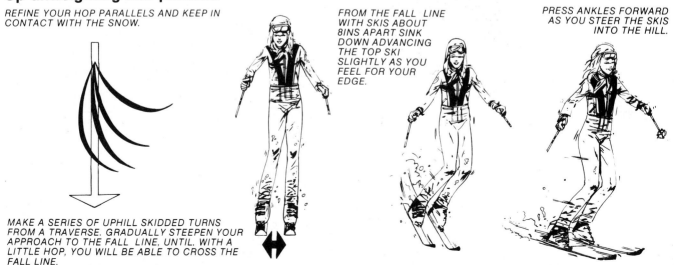

FROM THE FALL LINE WITH SKIS ABOUT 8INS APART SINK DOWN ADVANCING THE TOP SKI SLIGHTLY AS YOU FEEL FOR YOUR EDGE.

PRESS ANKLES FORWARD AS YOU STEER THE SKIS INTO THE HILL.

MAKE A SERIES OF UPHILL SKIDDED TURNS FROM A TRAVERSE. GRADUALLY STEEPEN YOUR APPROACH TO THE FALL LINE, UNTIL, WITH A LITTLE HOP, YOU WILL BE ABLE TO CROSS THE FALL LINE.

Parallels with a check

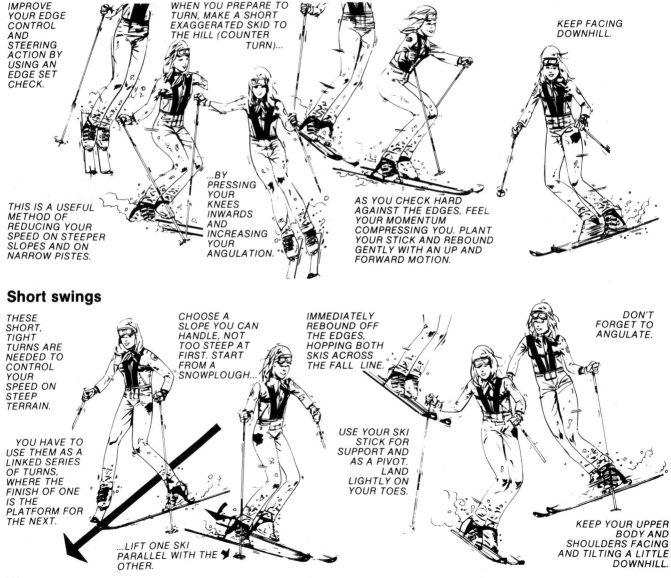

IMPROVE YOUR EDGE CONTROL AND STEERING ACTION BY USING AN EDGE SET CHECK.

WHEN YOU PREPARE TO TURN, MAKE A SHORT EXAGGERATED SKID TO THE HILL (COUNTER TURN)...

KEEP FACING DOWNHILL.

...BY PRESSING YOUR KNEES INWARDS AND INCREASING YOUR ANGULATION.

THIS IS A USEFUL METHOD OF REDUCING YOUR SPEED ON STEEPER SLOPES AND ON NARROW PISTES.

AS YOU CHECK HARD AGAINST THE EDGES, FEEL YOUR MOMENTUM COMPRESSING YOU. PLANT YOUR STICK AND REBOUND GENTLY WITH AN UP AND FORWARD MOTION.

Short swings

THESE SHORT, TIGHT TURNS ARE NEEDED TO CONTROL YOUR SPEED ON STEEP TERRAIN.

CHOOSE A SLOPE YOU CAN HANDLE, NOT TOO STEEP AT FIRST. START FROM A SNOWPLOUGH...

IMMEDIATELY REBOUND OFF THE EDGES, HOPPING BOTH SKIS ACROSS THE FALL LINE.

DON'T FORGET TO ANGULATE.

YOU HAVE TO USE THEM AS A LINKED SERIES OF TURNS, WHERE THE FINISH OF ONE IS THE PLATFORM FOR THE NEXT.

USE YOUR SKI STICK FOR SUPPORT AND AS A PIVOT. LAND LIGHTLY ON YOUR TOES.

...LIFT ONE SKI PARALLEL WITH THE OTHER.

KEEP YOUR UPPER BODY AND SHOULDERS FACING AND TILTING A LITTLE DOWNHILL.

Skiing over bumps

EVERYWHERE YOU SKI YOU'LL MEET BUMPY TERRAIN.

BUMPS AND HOLLOWS ARE USEFUL TO SKIERS WHO KNOW HOW TO USE THEM.

AS YOUR SKI TIP HITS A BUMP, BEND YOUR LEGS BY RAISING YOUR KNEES TOWARDS YOUR CHEST.

EXTEND YOUR LEGS IN THE HOLLOWS

TRY TO KEEP YOUR HEAD ALWAYS AT THE SAME LEVEL.

WHEN SCHUSSING OR TRAVERSING OVER BUMPS YOUR LEGS ARE YOUR SUSPENSION.

Turning on the moguls

MOGULS ARE ROUNDED BUMPS OF SNOW FORMED BY SKIERS TURNING CONTINUALLY. IT IS EASY TO TURN ON A MOGUL; JUST TURN YOUR LEGS, IN WHAT IS CALLED A "COMPRESSION TURN", OR "WELLEN" IN AUSTRIA, "AVALEMENT" IN FRANCE AND "ASSORBAMENTO" IN ITALY.

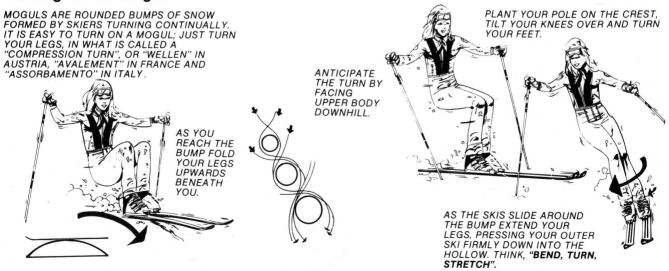

AS YOU REACH THE BUMP FOLD YOUR LEGS UPWARDS BENEATH YOU.

ANTICIPATE THE TURN BY FACING UPPER BODY DOWNHILL.

PLANT YOUR POLE ON THE CREST, TILT YOUR KNEES OVER AND TURN YOUR FEET.

AS THE SKIS SLIDE AROUND THE BUMP EXTEND YOUR LEGS, PRESSING YOUR OUTER SKI FIRMLY DOWN INTO THE HOLLOW. THINK, **"BEND, TURN, STRETCH"**.

Choosing the right terrain

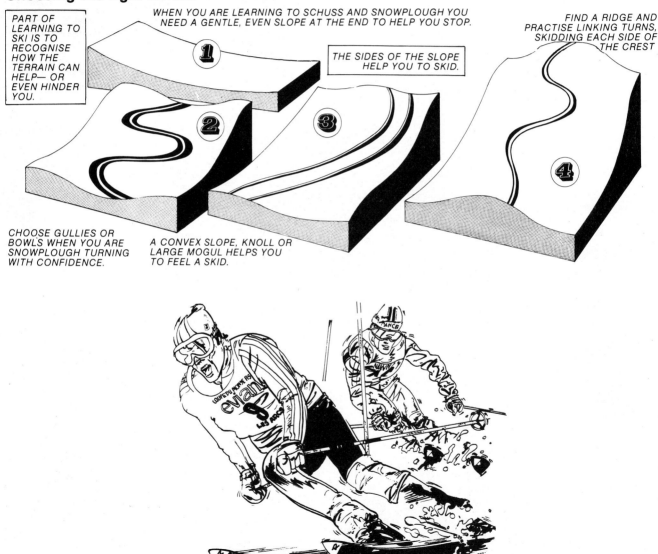

PART OF LEARNING TO SKI IS TO RECOGNISE HOW THE TERRAIN CAN HELP— OR EVEN HINDER YOU.

WHEN YOU ARE LEARNING TO SCHUSS AND SNOWPLOUGH YOU NEED A GENTLE, EVEN SLOPE AT THE END TO HELP YOU STOP.

THE SIDES OF THE SLOPE HELP YOU TO SKID.

FIND A RIDGE AND PRACTISE LINKING TURNS, SKIDDING EACH SIDE OF THE CREST

CHOOSE GULLIES OR BOWLS WHEN YOU ARE SNOWPLOUGH TURNING WITH CONFIDENCE.

A CONVEX SLOPE, KNOLL OR LARGE MOGUL HELPS YOU TO FEEL A SKID.

FITNESS AND PREPARATION FOR SKIING

Skiing, especially at high altitudes and in cold weather, makes considerable demands on your body. You need to be ski-fit. It's therefore important to prepare yourself well in advance. At least a couple of months before you go begin to build up your stamina and strength with regular exercises. Just as important is building up your flexibility. This will make you more agile and reduce your chances of accidental injury in a fall. Follow the programme of exercises suggested in this chapter and you will be able to make the most of your ski course or holiday.

When you are on the slopes, remember to drink lots of water, or water-based drinks, to replenish fluids lost in the dry mountain air. Eat well and get plenty of sleep.

Many old villages have retained their charm, while becoming modern ski resorts.

The importance of fitness

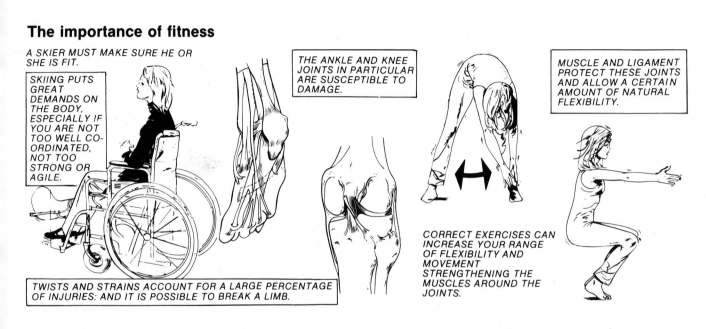

A SKIER MUST MAKE SURE HE OR SHE IS FIT.

SKIING PUTS GREAT DEMANDS ON THE BODY, ESPECIALLY IF YOU ARE NOT TOO WELL CO-ORDINATED, NOT TOO STRONG OR AGILE.

THE ANKLE AND KNEE JOINTS IN PARTICULAR ARE SUSCEPTIBLE TO DAMAGE.

MUSCLE AND LIGAMENT PROTECT THESE JOINTS AND ALLOW A CERTAIN AMOUNT OF NATURAL FLEXIBILITY.

CORRECT EXERCISES CAN INCREASE YOUR RANGE OF FLEXIBILITY AND MOVEMENT STRENGTHENING THE MUSCLES AROUND THE JOINTS.

TWISTS AND STRAINS ACCOUNT FOR A LARGE PERCENTAGE OF INJURIES: AND IT IS POSSIBLE TO BREAK A LIMB.

General training schedule

SKIING IS VERY STRENUOUS — SO YOU NEED TO BE A LOT FITTER THAN AVERAGE MEN AND WOMEN WHO SPEND MOST OF THEIR TIME EITHER SITTING OR SLEEPING. START TAKING EXTRA EXERCISE REGULARLY AT LEAST THREE MONTHS BEFORE YOU GO SKIING.

CYCLING

JOGGING

SKIPPING

RUNNING ON THE SPOT

IMMEDIATELY AFTER YOUR EXERCISES FEEL YOUR PULSE. IF IT IS UNDER 120 PER MINUTE YOU'RE NOT WORKING HARD ENOUGH.

Becoming ski-fit

A SKIER NEEDS TO BE SKI FIT.

SQUAT JUMPS

AT THE SAME TIME AS ACHIEVING A LEVEL OF GENERAL FITNESS YOU SHOULD BUILD UP THE STRENGTH AND ENDURANCE OF THE MUSCLES USED IN SKIING.

REVERSE ARM PRESS-UPS

SIT-UPS

A CANOEIST REQUIRES STRONG ARMS, BACK AND SHOULDER MUSCLES. HE MAY BE FIT FOR CANOEING, BUT IS HE FIT FOR SKIING?

Ski-fitness training

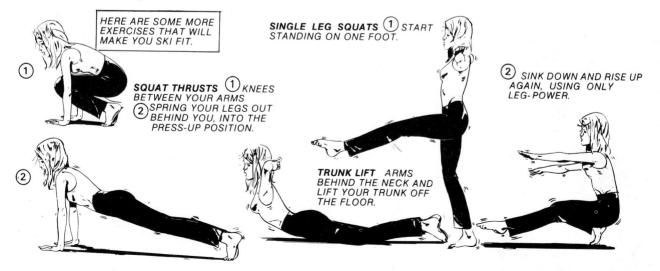

HERE ARE SOME MORE EXERCISES THAT WILL MAKE YOU SKI FIT.

SQUAT THRUSTS (1) *KNEES BETWEEN YOUR ARMS* (2) *SPRING YOUR LEGS OUT BEHIND YOU, INTO THE PRESS-UP POSITION.*

SINGLE LEG SQUATS (1) *START STANDING ON ONE FOOT.*

(2) *SINK DOWN AND RISE UP AGAIN, USING ONLY LEG-POWER.*

TRUNK LIFT *ARMS BEHIND THE NECK AND LIFT YOUR TRUNK OFF THE FLOOR.*

Flexibility and mobility exercises

THESE EXERCISES ARE DESIGNED TO INCREASE YOUR RANGE OF MOVEMENT IN CERTAIN JOINTS. DON'T ATTEMPT ANY OF THEM WITHOUT A WARM UP FIRST. MAKE ALL MOVEMENTS BY 'PRESSING' FIRMLY— NEVER JERK OR SWING.

SHOULDER STRETCH — PRESS YOUR ARMS BACK AS FAR AS YOU CAN, PALMS OF THE HANDS FACING OUTWARDS, HOLD IT AND RELAX, PRESS BACK FURTHER.

FRONTAL STRETCH — KEEP HIPS ON FLOOR, HOLD POSITION FOR 10 SECONDS. RELAX AND REPEAT.

BACK AND HAMSTRING STRETCH — RELAX BACK, REACH FOR LEFT TOE, THEN BETWEEN YOUR FEET, THEN YOUR RIGHT TOE.

More flexibility exercises

HIP STRETCH — SLOWLY TRY TO SIT DOWN ON THE FLOOR BETWEEN YOUR FEET.

DON'T FORGET TO PRESS SMOOTHLY — NO JERKY MOVEMENTS.

HIP AND KNEE CIRCLING — KEEP FEET HIP WIDTH APART, MOVE HIPS (THEN KNEES) IN AS LARGE A CIRCLE AS POSSIBLE AND KEEP YOUR HEAD DIRECTLY OVER YOUR FEET.

THIGH, HIP AND ABDOMINAL STRETCH — LUNGE POSITION, PRESS YOUR HIPS DOWN AS LOW AS YOU CAN.

Exercises to make you ski-fit.

Artificial ski slopes

You can race, practise ballet or just ski all the year round at the many artificial slopes now established throughout the UK. The techniques are exactly the same as for skiing on snow although the surface tends to be a little slower. Most artificial slopes offer practice periods, at certain times of the day, as well as ski courses and private lessons with qualified instructors.

Training on artificial slopes

IN GREAT BRITAIN THERE ARE OVER 70 ARTIFICIAL SKI SLOPES. ALL OF THESE PROVIDE INSTRUCTION BY QUALIFIED INSTRUCTORS.

YOU CAN LEARN NEARLY AS MUCH IN 8-12 HOURS INSTRUCTION ON PLASTIC SLOPES AS YOU CAN IN A FEW DAYS' HOLIDAY ON SNOW.

IN EFFECT, YOU CAN LEARN TO SKI BEFORE YOU REACH THE SNOW.

MOST ARTIFICIAL SLOPES HAVE A SKI AND/OR RACING CLUB WITH REGULAR MEETS AND COMPETITIONS...THESE HELP REGULAR SKIERS TO KEEP IN TRIM AND CONTINUE DEVELOPING THEIR SKILLS.

Types of artificial slopes

ARTIFICIAL SKI SLOPES ARE MADE OF SYNTHETIC FIBRE BRISTLES, SOMETHING LIKE A TOOTHBRUSH.

NO ARTIFICIAL SLOPES LOOK, SOUND OR FEEL MUCH LIKE SNOW!

MOST ARTIFICIAL SLOPES ARE MADE OF A MATERIAL CALLED SNO SLOPE MADE BY DENDIX, INCLUDING GLOUCESTER SKI SLOPE (THE LARGEST IN ENGLAND) AND HILLEND, NEAR EDINBURGH, AND PONTYPOOL IN WALES.

The National Coaching Scheme

The Coaching Scheme was introduced in 1977 and is administered under the auspices of the National Ski Federation of Great Britain by the English Ski Council and the Ski Council of Wales. It has been designed to cater for performers, coaches and officials.

A group ballet exhibition of a Royale turn.

Performers Skiers who wish either to develop their proficiency, or to compete in one of the disciplines — Alpine, or Nordic skiing.

Coaches The core of the organisation is the Coach Award Scheme, designed to provide training for potential instructors up to coach level. The Coach Award covers three categories — recreational, racing and freestyle. The standard required to become a trainee instructor is to be able to perform the following in a skilful manner:

Direct side slip — at least five metres to both sides

Forward diagonal side skid — from a traverse skid at least three metres to both sides

Swing to hill — from the fall line to both sides

Parallel turns — a minimum of six linked parallel turns

Elementary slalom — two separate descents making continuous linked turns through gates, over a minimum distance of 40 metres

Officials Skiers and those involved in the organisation of competitions, who wish to qualify as race officials, freestyle judges, referees and other officials

Registration You can register with the Coaching Scheme and receive newsletters and correspondence about it. For further details you can obtain the Coaching Scheme Booklet, price 50p from:—

The Coaching Secretary ESC, NSFGB, 118 Eaton Square, LONDON SW1W 9AF Tel. 01-235 8227

Ski schools

It is difficult to learn to ski on your own. You really need the help of experts if you are going to avoid developing bad habits, and succeed in becoming proficient as quickly as possible.

National Ski schools There is no single or ideal way to learn. Nearly all skiing countries have their own National Ski Schools and each endeavours to promote the idea that their teaching method is the best, the most effective and the quickest way to learn.

To avoid confusion it is best to concentrate on the fundamental aspects of technique described in this book. These are common to all ski schools, although the emphasis may vary from one to another.

Size of classes Fifteen is the absolute maximum that should be accepted in a ski class. In many cases the average is a little less than this number.

Recognise the experts Your instructors should be properly qualified and, if they are they will wear the badge of their National Ski School. In Italy the badge is a green, white and red bar, with *Maestro di Sci* on it. In Switzerland instructors' badges consists of a shield with the Swiss white cross on a red background. The Austrian badge is a background, crossed by a bar. *Staatlich geprüfter Schilehrer* is written on it. The British instructors have a shield shaped badge with a Union Jack and *British Ski Instructor* and *BASI* written on it. There is also a separate NSFGB badge for those qualified to teach on artificial ski slopes only.

Language barrier Most resorts frequented by British tour operators have local instructors who speak at least *some* English. Many speak it well. In an increasing number of resorts, particularly in Italy, you will find British instructors.

Ski proficiency tests

Proficiency Tests
At the end of a week's ski holiday you can measure your progress by taking a ski test. Most countries operate a badge system, but the standard of the tests vary from place to place. The Swiss provide a bronze, silver and gold medal. Although it may take some time to acquire a gold, the tests are well thought out and you can be sure you will have achieved something if you pass. If you aspire to be an instructor passing your proficiency test is the essential first step.

In Britain the National Ski Federation administer the ski tests. They can be taken on snow or artificial slopes. There are British Junior Alpine Ski tests available to all under 18.

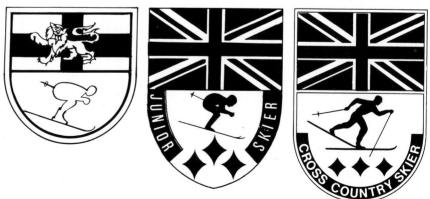

These badges are awarded by the English Ski Council and the National Ski Federation of Great Britain. The NSFGB badges have one star for a bronze test, two for a silver and three for a gold.

Glossary

Angulation
A forward bending at the hips, as the upper body tends to follow its momentum when the legs are turned to steer the skis.

Anti-friction pad
A small pad attached to the ski close to the toe piece, usually made of Teflon. Its function is to allow the boot to leave the ski when it is released in a fall.

Basic swing
Rhythmically linked turns with ploughed and skidded phases, which are used to learn the essential elements of parallel skiing.

Cable car
in German; Luftseilbahn
in French; Télépherique
in Italian; Funivia

Uphill transport consisting of a cabin suspended from an overhead cable.

Camber
The arch that is built into the ski enabling the skier's weight to be distributed along the entire running surface of the ski.

Canting
Altering the angle of the boot on the ski, in order to compensate for way individuals stand on skis.

Chair lift
in German; Sesselbahn
in French; Télésiège
in Italian; Seggiovia

Uphill transport consisting of double or single seater chairs suspended from an overhead cable. Skis can be worn or carried.

Check
A sudden, short skid, to check speed or in preparation for a turn.

Christiania (Christie)
A turn made with skis parallel. Named after the district now called Oslo in Norway.

Clock or star turn
A method of changing direction on the flat. Its name derives from the pattern left in the snow after a complete turn.

Compression turns
in German; Wellen
in French; Avalement
in Italian; Assorbamento

A turning technique in which the legs are turned whilst bending and extending to keep a constant pressure between the soles of the skis and the snow.

Drag lift
An overhead cable system with attachments by which skiers are pulled up a slope. Variations are the poma or button lift, and the T-bar designed for two persons to travel side by side.

Edging
The lateral tilting of the skis towards the slope. Used to control the sideways movement of the skis.

Edge change
Changing from one set of edges to the other in order to effect a change of direction.

Egg position
A crouched position used in racing to minimise wind resistance.

Fall line
The imaginary line which follows the steepest gradient of a slope.

FIS
Federation Internationale de Ski, the international governing body of skiing.

Föhn
A warm wind which blows onto the Alps from the south.

Foot steer
The sensation of steering the ski with the foot, when the leg is rotated around an axis which passes through the ball of the foot.

GLM
Graduated Length Method. A method of ski teaching using short skis at first and progressing to longer skis as ability improves. Ski Evolutif is a similar method developed in France.

Heel piece
Part of the release binding that clasps the heel of the boot to the ski.

Herringbone
A climbing step with skis in a V-shape open at the tips. The name derives from the pattern left in the snow.

Inside ski
The ski on the inside of the turning arc.

Kick turn
Changing direction through 180° in a standing position across a slope.

Kilometro Lanciato
The Flying Kilometre. The annual competition to attack the world speed record on the upper slopes of Cervinia, Italy.

Lapse rate
The rate at which the temperature drops as you gain altitude.

Linked turns
Continuous turning down a slope where one turn leads straight into the next.

Loipe
Marked trail for cross country skiers.

Lower ski
The ski on the downhill side of the slope.

Moguls
Large rounded bumps on the ski slope formed sometimes by the terrain under the snow but usually by the action of many skiers turning repeatedly in the same place.

Nursery slopes
Gentle gradients where beginners first learn to ski.

Outside ski
The ski on the outside of the turning arc.

Parallel skiing
Edges are changed simultaneously, whilst turning and skis are parallel throughout the descent.

Piste
Marked and prepared ski runs.

Release bindings
The mechanisms which secure the boot to the skis. They are designed to release the boots at a pre-determined pressure. The adjustments which determine the point of release must be made in relation to the skill, weight, strength and size of the skier.

Retaining strap
Strap attached to binding and skier to stop the ski running away after it has been released (see also Ski stopper).

Schuss
Straight running down the fall line with skis parallel.

Short swings
Used on steeper terrain; short quick turns with pronounced edge set helping to control downhill speed.

Side slip
A sideways movement of the skis due to release of edges and the pull of gravity.

Side skid
A sideways movement of the skis when edged and turned across the direction of the momentum of the skier.

Side stepping
A climbing step with skis on their uphill edges horizontally across the fall line.

Ski patrol
The organisation responsible for policing the ski area. They are concerned with safety on the pistes, ambulancing and directing ski traffic.

Ski stopper
A sprung mechanical device which operates to prevent the ski from running down the hill when the boot is released from the binding.

Slalom
Controlled downhill skiing between gates. These are pairs of red and blue flags. Giant slalom is a faster version of special slalom.

Snowploughing
Basic skiing technique with skis held in a V-shape, heels apart and skidding against the inside edges.

Stem
Action of moving one ski from a parallel position to an angled position. Movement which enables a skier to start an elementary turn, from a traverse or diagonal skid.

Traverse
Movement across a slope holding a line.

Unweighting
Moving the body in relation to the skis to bring about a reduction of weight between skis and snow. Unweighting facilitates edge change and turning the skis.

Wedeln
Continuous rhythmical linked turns close to the fall line with very little edge set.

The Author

John Shedden is currently the top authority
on ski coaching in Britain. He first went skiing
on a school visit at the age of 15 and was so
taken with the sport that he made his own skis
when he returned home. Later he was to
become a ski instructor in Scotland and he
trained in Austria as a State Ski Teacher,
before becoming Assistant National Coach for
the National Ski Federation of Great Britain.
Since then he has qualified as a teacher of
physical education and written several books,
become Director of Coaching to the English
Ski Council of the NSFGB and a member of
the Federation Internationale de Ski
committee for children and youth skiing.

58